PRAISE FOR *Italian Folk Magic*

"Mary-Grace Fahrun's *Italian Folk Magic* is an intimate journey into the heart of Italian folk magical practices as they are lived every day. Having grown up in an extended Italian family in North America and Italy, the author presents us with the stories, characters, saints, charms, and prayers that form the core of folk religion, setting them in context in an authentic, down-to-earth, and humorous voice. A delight to read!"
—Sabina Magliocco, professor of anthropology,
University of British Columbia

"Mary-Grace Fahrun's *Italian Folk Magic* is a tribute to Italian mothers and grandmothers who kept their loved ones well fed and in good health with recipes and remedies concocted from their magical kitchens."
—Agata De Santis, director of the documentary
film *Mal'occhio*, founder of *italocanadese.com*

"This is an extraordinary book, a divine gift from Italian ancestors full of ordinary ways to live an enchanted life. In revealing 'folk magic' practiced and passed down through generations, Mary-Grace tells favorite family stories, opening the door for readers to enter the magical world in which she lives, wherein we discover our own. My Polish soul fell in love with these Italian sisters and the wisdom they reveal and will do so evermore as I make their magic. In any collection of books on magic, *Italian Folk Magic* belongs on the top shelf."
—Karol Jackowski, author of
Sister Karol's Book of Spells and Blessings

"*Italian Folk Magic* is a charming, honest, and practical insight into an area of witchcraft that's often been overwrought with unnecessary outside influences. If you gather at the hearth of the Italian household, you will find a beautiful practice that doesn't require the dressing of ceremonial magic or recreated rites. Through the author's family tales, I was transported back to my own childhood memories of my Italian family in South Philadelphia. While magic traditions will definitely differ from family to family, region to region, there are underlying threads that are strikingly familiar that will speak to every reader. Through stories of recipes, superstitions, saints, and more, Mary-Grace serves up a delightful dish of a book that speaks to the heart of Italian witchcraft practices. Truly inspiring and a wonderful read!"

—Laura Tempest Zakroff, author of
Sigil Witchery: A Witch's Guide to Crafting Magick Symbols and
The Witch's Cauldron: The Craft, Lore and Magick of Ritual Vessels

"There has been little written on Italian folk magic throughout the years, possibly because many who perform folk magic do not think of what they are doing as magic. Mary-Grace Fahrun's book beautifully illustrates how magic never died and has continued to be practiced by European peoples. It shows that instead of magic being a fantasy lying outside of the mundane world, it was interfused with the everyday, enchanting every aspect of life with its great mystery. Folk magic is reenchanting the world again, through Italian proverbs and recipes in this book, intimately intertwined with the culture and families of Italian descent. This is a beautiful thing to see in the written word."

—Marcus R. McCoy, cofounder of the Viridis
Genii symposium and perfumer at House of Orpheus

"Whether you are of Italian ancestry or not, *Italian Folk Magic* is a great practical book full of history, culture, recipes, remedies, insight, magic, and more, which is sure to effect and shape your perspective on witchcraft and your everyday life. Rue enthusiastically invigorates a waning layer of folk tradition with a burst of momentum for a burgeoning generation of folk magic practitioners."

—Christopher Orapello, artist,
coauthor of *Besom, Stang, and Sword* and
cohost of the podcast, *Down at the Crossroads*

Italian Folk Magic

Rue's
Kitchen
Witchery

Mary-Grace Fahrun

Foreword by Andrea Romanazzi, PhD

WEISER BOOKS

For Brigid and Brenna

This edition first published in 2018 by Weiser Books, an imprint of
Red Wheel/Weiser, LLC
With offices at:
65 Parker Street, Suite 7
Newburyport, MA 01950
www.redwheelweiser.com

ISBN: 978-1-57863-618-1
Library of Congress Cataloging-in-Publication Data
available upon request

Cover design by Jim Warner
Interior by Steve Amarillo / Urban Design LLC
Typeset in Adobe Mrs Eaves and Mighty Script
Printed in Canada
MAR
10 9 8 7 6 5

TABLE OF CONTENTS

This book contains advice and information relating to herbs and is not meant to diagnose, treat, or prescribe. It should be used to supplement, not replace, the advice of your physician or other trained health-care practitioner. Some herbs are poisonous and should be used with extreme care. If you know or suspect you have a medical condition, if you are experiencing physical symptoms, or if you feel unwell, seek your physician's advice before embarking on any medical program or treatment. Readers using the information in this book do so entirely at their own risk, and the author and publisher accept no liability if adverse effects are caused.

Foreword

I was very honored when I was asked to review Mary-Grace Fahrun's first book and happy to discover how, in the US, among the families of Italian immigrants, the red thread of memory that binds them to magical Italy was never severed. It is in this manner that I entered Mary-Grace's beautiful kitchen. In Italy, especially in the past, the kitchen was the most important room. Here the women put into practice all their knowledge handed down from mother to daughter through millennia, not only aimed at the stove, but also and above all, magical. The kitchen was the place where children were raised, stories and legends were told, the magic of herbs was taught, and where natural medicines, ointments, and potions were prepared. Since time immemorial, the ancient knowledge of the Ancestors was shared around the fire. I therefore entered Mary-Grace's kitchen and I stopped to watch and listen.

Already from the preface, I felt part of the family warmth: listening to the stories of the aunts and uncles, smelling the aroma of fried pizza dough, macaroni with sauce, the shuffle of playing cards, strictly Neapolitan. I, too, born in 1974 in Bari, a city in the south of Italy in the region of Puglia, witnessed firsthand that magic that was lived and breathed at my grandparents' house. But just as in Mary-Grace's kitchen, there was not only the profane. Small altars were present everywhere. I remember that my grandmother always lit a candle before the image of the Madonna while a picture of Saint Joseph resided within the *madia*—the wooden box inside which the bread was kept. My grandmother back then, like Mary-Grace today, would describe to me how to make these small and sacred altars, with simplicity but, at the same time, with magic.

Yes, magic, because behind the figures of dozens of Christian saints were hundreds of Pagan gods, veiled but never forgotten, in a mixture of images and symbols associated with the aforementioned saints: holy icons, red horns, horseshoes, various amulets, and candles. My grandmother taught me all that was hidden behind her every motion; here was born my passion for Italian witchcraft. Just like Mary-Grace today, between a plate of *minestra* (soup) and one of *pasta asciutta* (pasta), she talked to me about the traditions and the annual festivals. She told me tales of magic, as for example her meeting with the *lupomino* (the werewolf), the "Fairy of the house," of the magic of Nature that can heal or punish. I found all this in Mary-Grace's kitchen, and for this I want to compliment her.

Beautiful is the section dedicated to the Proverbs, a term that derives from the Latin, *pro-verbo* (through the word). It is precisely through the word that sound is transformed into music, incantation, or spell and therefore magic. Here are the many incantations, those that had purposes of blessing and healing, but also attacking and defending. Repeatedly whispering words incomprehensible to untrained ears—this is what was in the kitchen and on the dining table, where the grandmother removed the evil eye with her shallow bowl full of water in which she poured three drops of oil or uttered the spell to chase away a child's tummy pains:

"U lenedeia sante, u martedeia sante, u merqueledeia sante, u scevedeia sante, u venerdeia sante, u sàbbate sante, demeneche iè Pasque, u vèrme ntèrra casche."

"Holy Monday, Holy Tuesday, Holy Wednesday, Holy Thursday, Holy Friday, Holy Saturday, Easter Sunday, the worm falls to the ground."

I find all this in Mary-Grace's beautiful and cozy kitchen. Stories, legends, cooking recipes, spells, tips, oracular techniques, and then the Lotto, the game of our grandparents, but also of today: "29, 86, 26 . . . go immediately to play them!"

This was and is Magic, not the neo-pagan traditions on the rise that attempt a legacy or heritage, by whatever means, that they do not possess, but the ancient and powerful Italian magic of the countryside, the place where you can still hear the voices of the Ancestors between the sacred and the profane. This is Mary-Grace's magic! This is her "kitchen"! Therefore read this book, enter its rooms, listen to its proverbs, its advice on how to create sacred places, do magic. Use it as an almanac. Punctuate time with it. Relish it.

—Andrea Romanazzi, PhD, author of
La Stregoneria in Italia: scongiuri, amuleti e riti della tradizione
and *Guida alle Streghe in Italia*

Bari, Italy
December 25, 2017

Preface

The Eye

Saturday night was my favorite night growing up. We would arrive at my aunt and uncle's house around three in the afternoon. The table would already be set with bowls of nuts, olives, and lupini beans. The sweet and yeasty aroma of rising dough filled the kitchen. I could hardly contain my excitement. I knew this aroma meant my zia would be making pizza and *pizza fritta* soon. Everyone would sit at the kitchen table—the uncles at one end, playing *briscola* or *Tre-Sette*; the aunts at the other end, sharing the latest sewing project.

Then there was me. A very observant six-year-old, I picked the best seat in the house. I sat right in the middle of the long table between the aunts on one side and the uncles on the other. I would sit there for hours. I would watch my uncles play cards. I watched very closely—learning the card games and then playing them against myself with a spare deck of Neapolitan cards. I observed very intently. I knew which uncles cheated. I would make eye contact, and that uncle would wink at me to not reveal our secret. There was always five or ten dollars in it for me. In hindsight, I realize the stakes were quite high for me to get five to ten dollars just for keeping a secret. It was 1974.

My aunt's house was always full of people on Saturdays. The front door opened and closed all day as people dropped in to visit. Some would stay awhile, have a drink and something to eat, and then go. Others would come and stay the whole day, well into the wee hours of Sunday morning.

I'm an only child. My cousins were all at least five years older than me and allowed to go to the park to play. My older cousins, the ones that were of legal age, would come to grab a bite to eat and ask their parents for money and to borrow the car on their way to the discotheque. That was fine by me. I was used to the company of adults. As long as I was quiet, they didn't mind or even notice I was there.

On one particular Saturday, one of the neighbors, Signora Cristina, dropped in. I had never seen Signora Cristina in person, but I did hear her name mentioned in conversations. My aunts would always drop their voices down to a whisper when they mentioned her. There was always one aunt who would say, "Sssshhh . . . don't say her name," and they would either cross themselves or touch their gold jewelry.

Compared to my aunts, Signora Cristina looked like a movie star. Her jet black hair was in an updo that looked like a cross between a beehive and a French twist. Her big brown eyes were rimmed with black kohl, and she had the longest, blackest eyelashes I had ever seen. Two thin, very large, hoop earrings hung from each ear. She wore a baby blue dress, and her nails were painted the same shiny blood red as her lipstick. She wore a lot of jewelry. Every finger had at least one ring on it. Her perfume, Tigress by Fabergé—she would tell me when I asked—filled the kitchen, overwhelming even the huge cloud of cigarette smoke from my uncles. Then she reached into her purse and spritzed some on my wrists! I could not take my eyes off her. She was so beautiful, and her voice was a little deeper and softer than any of my aunts'. She opened her purse and pulled out a long cigarette from a silver box. My uncle Federico quickly jumped to offer her a light, and my aunt Nella, his wife, shot him a dirty look.

My cousin Marina, who was eighteen, came to the table to get a cigarette from her mom's, my aunt Nella's, pack. When Marina put her hand down on the package, Signora Cristina quickly snatched her hand and pulled her toward her. "Mamma mia, let me look at you! You are so beautiful. Your hair, so thick and jet black. I have to dye mine now, and half of it is a wig! And your skin, my God, how I wish my skin still looked like that. But you're too thin. Men want meat; bones they throw to the dog!"

Meanwhile, I could hear my aunt Nella calling, "Marina," to get her attention. I looked over at my aunt Nella, and from the look on her face, I could tell that she really didn't like Signora Cristina. Suddenly, the phone rang and my cousin Marina ran to answer it.

After about thirty minutes or so, the doorbell rang. A man was at the door, and Signora Cristina had to go. My uncles looked at each other and chuckled. My aunts looked at my uncles and each other and frowned.

A couple hours later, it was just me and my aunts in the kitchen. My uncles had all moved to the living room to watch the hockey game. My cousin Marina came back to the kitchen. She sat in a chair just across the table from me. My aunt Nella asked her if she had eaten. She said no, she wasn't hungry. She looked pale and sweaty and was complaining to my aunt Nella that her head and her left eye hurt. I looked over at my cousin, and her face was white as a sheet. Her left eye began to swell, and Marina just went limp in her chair. She couldn't keep her head up. Her head kept falling backward, and her speech was slurred.

Suddenly, I heard one of my aunts call, "Nella! Look at Marina!" My aunt Nella stubbed out her cigarette in the nearest ashtray and grabbed her daughter Marina's head in her hands to look at her face.

"That whore. I knew it. She put the eye on my daughter."

I was sitting at the table not knowing what the first word meant, and who and how someone put another eye on my cousin.

My aunt Nella did the sign of the cross on herself three times (so did all my other aunts at the table) and kissed the eighteen-karat gold crucifix hanging on the thin gold chain around her neck as she grabbed a shallow bowl and put some water from the sink in it and placed it on the table in front of my cousin, who looked like she was asleep on her chair. My aunt dropped olive oil into the bowl of water. She said words that sounded Italian to me but I didn't recognize. Then she took two knives and begun cutting the water and oil in the bowl. Now all my aunts were quietly praying to San Michele (Saint Michael Archangel) to cast out the evil. My aunt Nella's sister grabbed a handful of salt and sprinkled it around the kitchen floor. Another aunt grabbed the broom and swept the kitchen and then swept the salt and dust out the back door at the other end of the kitchen. My aunt Nella then grabbed the bowl, spat in it, and tossed the contents out the back door. Her sister picked up a long black hair stuck to the chair Signora Cristina had occupied and placed it carefully onto a paper napkin. She folded it neatly and tucked it in the pocket of my aunt Nella's apron. My godmother asked me if Signora Cristina gave me anything. I said, "No, she just put some perfume on my wrists." Before I could finish my sentence, my godmother lunged at me and whisked me over to the sink to wash my hands and wrists.

When I turned to look at my cousin Marina, she was sitting up in her chair, and the swollen eye had gone back to normal. Her mother was handing her a tiny glass of wine. "Drink some blessed wine, Marina, to get rid of anything that may still be inside you." Then everything went back to normal. My cousin took off to go dancing with her friends, and my aunts began frying the dough to make pizza fritta.

Definition of Italian Witchcraft Practice

First, I need to make one thing perfectly clear: never in a million years would anyone present that night *ever* describe their practice as *stregoneria* (witchcraft). Nor would any respectable member of my family or community *ever* self-identify as a *strega* (witch). Never. Occasionally, taken off-guard, they may have implied it. However, if asked about it later, they would categorically deny it. At the very most, they would perhaps admit to being superstitious. In all my learning, and for lack of a better word, apprenticeship, under the matriarchs of my family and community, even if someone in our community was a known *maga* or *mago* (practitioners of magic), no one would ever utter their name when speaking about them. Very much like in those famous books about the boy wizard where no one speaks the name of his mortal enemy.

When I speak of my learning and apprenticeship, it isn't what you imagine. I didn't attend daily witch lessons. I was raised very much like an orphan—by a community made up of Italian and Italian immigrant relatives, friends, and neighbors. I grew up in a time and in a family where all importance was placed on raising girls to be good housewives. Being a good housewife meant learning every skill required to maintain and run a household and a family. Good housewives, or *femmine di casa* (in Italian dialect), were responsible for maintaining all the practices, customs, and traditions of our family and village of origin. All this while often working forty hours per week in a factory or sweat shop.

From a very young age, I fell in line. I learned to cook, sew, embroider, garden, do laundry, etc. It was common in my neighborhood for young girls as young as eight years old to rush home after school to clean and get supper started before their mothers arrived home from work. We were told that this was all to make us good wives.

I never really felt aligned with the Italian dream of getting married and having children. Certainly not when I was still a child myself. At the age of sixteen, I began to rebel against what I described as the "patriarchal indoctrination and subjugation of women."

That summer I landed my first paying job and learned to drive. I had no intention of being anyone's housewife ever. Heck, I didn't even want to be Italian anymore because being Italian meant having to give up my dreams and be confined in what I felt was an archaic social construct. I was born in America, and therefore, I was born free! Two years later when I turned eighteen, I struck out on my own, putting all that useless domestic training behind me. Why not? I was never going to use any of it anyway.

Or so I thought.

You see, I thought all I was being taught was to cook and clean when, in fact, the education I received was so much more profound than home economics. I thought I was walking away from all this in the summer of 1986. Instead, I was heading down a path that would take me to what would become my life's work of love.

What I learned at the feet of the great matriarchs of my family and community was the Italian language and a number of diverse dialects. Each one of them spoke the dialect of their home town in Italy. I learned about where my people came from and who they were—and by extension where I came from. I learned about our history, customs, and tradition.

I learned that our tradition is very rich, and that it contains magical and religious rituals and prayers for the outward expression of our inner spirituality for every phase and condition of our lives. The practices of witchcraft, folk medicine, blessing rituals, cooking, and crafting are inextricably woven into the fabric of Italian culture—no matter where Italians are geographically located. Together, these components make up a beautiful tapestry unique to each practitioner. Together, these components are vastly greater, and more intangible, than the sum of their parts; thus, from both the practical and cultural standpoint, any effort to divorce one from the other diminishes the tradition as a whole.

Like I said, I didn't attend witch lessons, and the witchcraft is inextricably woven into the fabric. . . . You get the gist. There's a Zen proverb: "After enlightenment, the laundry." I'm not Zen, I'm Italian, so I was thinking of doing it this way: "After the laundry, enlightenment." Meaning, I want to share with you my personal knowledge and experience of all the above-mentioned components of Italian witchcraft. My hope is you then take these components, do your own research, and craft a tapestry of practice that is uniquely you.

Language and Place of Origin

I am fluent in Italian, including five or six regional dialects. My mother was from northern Italy, my father from central Italy. I grew up in a family and a neighborhood made up of mainly central and southern Italian immigrants. We spoke Italian dialects at home, in the schoolyard, and at the supermarket. I attended Saturday morning Italian school and attended Italian Roman Catholic Mass almost every Sunday. Okay, maybe not. We attended Mass mainly on holidays and sacraments. Okay, we didn't attend Mass regularly. I digress.

My family always talked about the region of Italy they came from and their hometown. Always. I grew up listening to the same stories over and over again. Now that my parents are gone, I have memories of their lives growing up that are almost more vivid than my own!

The reason I bring up language is that I was taught everything in Italian. The dialect varied from zia to nonna, but the message was always clear. Not because I was fluent, but because I was interested, and when I wasn't interested, because of repetition.

If you don't already know about your family's region of Italy and their hometown, research it. Learn the history of the town, who the patron saint is, and any legends associated with it and the local cuisine and specialties. Cook something your nonna made you when you were little. Cook something your parents talked about enjoying when they were little. Talk to your family members and relatives. Connect with people whose ancestors hail from the same region and, if possible, town as yours did. My most favorite computer application in the entire world is the one where I can type in a location and view satellite and street-level images. I call it "visiting." I visited our *paese* in Italy in person when I was younger. Now I visit it using the aforementioned computer application. Seriously, it never ceases to fill me with awe.

What if you don't speak Italian? What? You don't speak Italian? What is wrong with you?! Just kidding. By the end of this book, I guarantee you will have a new appreciation for the language, and you may even pick up a few hundred words. I also highly recommend learning the language. We live in such an exciting time when we can learn a language for free from the comfort of our own home computer or phone app. You are of Italian ancestry with the genetic information of all those who came before you in your DNA. I assure you: it's in you. Learn the language so you can appreciate the wordplay in everyday things we take for granted, like why your favorite *maccheroni* (pasta) is called *penne* (or quills, because they look like quills) or *spaghetti* (little strings, because they look like pieces of string). Learn the language to pronounce it *espresso*, not *expresso*; and *bruschetta* [broo-sket'tah], not [brooshettah]; and to be honest, *gabagool* is not even a word. It is pronounced *capicollo*. . . . Learn the language so that your heart and mind can connect to your heritage.

What if you are not of Italian ancestry but inexplicably drawn to Italian witchcraft?

Let me answer this question with a little personal anecdote. My eldest daughter lives and breathes Japanese anime. She is not Japanese. She is Canadian of Italian, German, and Romanian ancestry. Her interest in

Japanese anime led to her learning anime culture and, by extension, a knowledge of how Japanese language differs from English language as evidenced by some pretty comical examples of translation. She has a decent knowledge of Japanese popular culture, some words, and of course, food and snacks. She surrounds herself with like-minded people who may not be Japanese, but who also live and breathe Japanese anime. They don't need to be or speak Japanese to be passionate about Japanese anime. See my point?

So what if you are not Italian? Immerse yourself and cultivate your interest in Italian witchcraft, and everything else will follow. Learn how to cook Italian food. If you're not into cooking, learn how to order Italian food at a restaurant. Learn the history. Learn the language. You don't need to be fluent. All you need is to be truly interested.

The last point I described in my Japanese anime anecdote is: find your tribe.

The aim is not to practice "authentic" Italian witchcraft. That's way too much pressure—even for me! That would imply that there is only one way. There is no such thing. Authentic how? There is no way I do things exactly the way my nonna did in the 1930s in her little mountain village in Italy. Nor do I do things exactly the way my nonna's sister did forty years later in America. I will share with you their practices. I will share with you my practice. A practice influenced and informed by those who came before me and shared their stories, skills, and secrets. The purpose of this book is to provide you with a guided tour of my magical life and introduce you to, and for some of you, reacquaint you with, the principles so you can create your own magical life. The Italian witchcraft I will be presenting is not a religion. It is a practice anyone can incorporate into their spirituality regardless of religious belief. However, there will be strong themes of devotions to saints and earth-based spirituality because they are both important to the fabric. In sharing with you these beautiful practices I am so passionate about and how they enrich my life, I hope to infect you with the same passion. May it, in turn, enrich your life, and you will become a member of my tribe.

Introduction

But there's a story behind everything. How a picture got on a wall. How a scar got on your face. Sometimes the stories are simple, and sometimes they are hard and heartbreaking. But behind all your stories is always your mother's story, because hers is where yours begin.

—Mitch Albom, For One More Day

People say necessity is the mother of invention, and I couldn't agree more. It was the summer of 1998. My father had been diagnosed with brain cancer at the young age of sixty-five. The matriarchs in my family were growing older and frailer by the minute. I was preparing to move from Montreal to Toronto because I had received a job offer there. I was at a personal crossroads, and the job market in Montreal was bleak, even for a registered nurse. I needed to take something with me more than just my personal belongings. I needed to take something of my roots.

I began to ask for recipes. I purchased a beautiful hardcover journal at my favorite dollar store. I would learn years later that the beautiful cover was a print of Dante Gabriele Rossetti's *A Sea Spell* (1877). I had no idea at that time where this recipe journal would take me!

I began by asking my mom, my aunts, my godmothers; my friends' moms, aunts, grandmothers, godmothers, etc. As recipes poured in, so did their stories. Visits and phone calls went longer and longer.

Over endless cups of black Italian coffee and all kinds of homemade cookies and cakes, cured meats and cheeses, and wine, I wrote it all down. When I didn't have my journal with me, I wrote on the back of envelopes and on paper napkins.

What was really interesting were the conversations that would evolve around the recipes. For example, one of my aunts, who was an amazing cook, warned: "But don't make this when you are on your period; it won't turn out." "But why?" I would ask. "Because there is too much power in your hands; it will ruin this delicate dish. During that time of the month, make *brodo* [broth] or braise tough meats. The power in your hands will toughen tender filet, but will tenderize the toughest meats." Then her voice dropped to a whisper: "Your other aunt is in menopause. That's why her *braciole* is so tough."

Now, having been raised by these people, I didn't think anything of their warnings. I was raised immersed in this culture. I was exposed to many regional variations of Italian culture, and because languages come easily to me, I learned the dialects effortlessly. Praying the rosary and burying a statue of Saint Joseph in the ground, head down, to sell a house, on the same day, was as normal as normal could be. Like when giving a compliment. We always followed a compliment with *s'a benedica* or *sci-bendette-Di* (both meaning "God bless"). Failing to do so would inadvertently give the receiver of the compliment *malocchio* (the evil eye). Worse, you would be perceived as doing so *on purpose*.

As I began saying, these same matriarchs weren't getting any younger. It seemed as though overnight, they had all become frail, and one by one they began to become ill and die. One evening, after attending a funeral, I happened to glance at my recipe journal on my kitchen table. I opened it up to the page with my recently deceased relative's *taralli* recipe. I ran my fingertips over her handwriting. It was hard to believe I had just pasted this into my book less than two weeks earlier. Remembering our conversation that began with taralli and digressed into spells "to find a good husband" made me smile. That is, until I couldn't remember one of the details and absentmindedly picked up the phone to call her. First, I was bewildered. Then, a deep sorrow washed over me. Just as I was ready to wallow in loss and grief, a new emotion showed its head. PANIC. I called one of my aunts and began blurting out: "Who is going to remember all these recipes when everyone is gone? Who will remember the stories and the things we do?" My aunt, now in her seventies, quietly replied: "You." Me? "Yeah. You. Don't panic," she said. " Do you have a paper and pen handy? I'll talk, you write."

This is the moment Rue's Kitchen was born. The matriarchs of my family and neighborhood came out of the woodwork to help me remember and write things down. Recipes, folk remedies, stories, superstitions, prayers, incantations, oh my. . . . Sometimes they were complete. Sometimes they were fragments. Most of the time they were in their regional dialect mixed with French and English.

In the summer of 1998, I began posting this information on an Internet message board dedicated to Italian Americans. I shared my ever-growing bank of recipes, customs, traditions, folklore, folk magic, superstitions, and so on. Other members shared theirs. At the same time, I started a web page. Literally one page about Italian witchcraft with my email address. Emails began to pour in. My web page quickly evolved into a website, as I uploaded more and more information.

In July 2000, my website turned two. The time had come for me to register my domain: *www.rueskitchen.com.* I can hardly believe how long ago that feels.

For those of you reading this who are not familiar with my website, here is what it says on my home page:

> Rue's Kitchen's primary mission is the preservation of customs and practices. Herein you will find traditional Italian (from various regions) witchcraft (stregoneria italiana), folk magic (magia operativa), folk medicine (medicina popolare tradizionale), and old-fashioned Roman Catholic folk religion, (scongiuri, congiuri ed incantesimi), practiced, by Italians of all faiths, all over the world. You will also find information on customs, traditions, and heirloom recipes.

Why "Rue's Kitchen"? The kitchen, my kitchen, has always been the hub of many charms, rituals, healings, and celebrations.

This tradition is very rich, and in it will be found the magical and religious rituals and prayers for the outward expression of one's inner spirituality for every phase and condition of one's life. The practices of witchcraft, folk medicine, blessing rituals, and cooking are inextricably woven into the fabric of Italian culture—no matter where Italians are geographically located. Together, these components are vastly greater, and more intangible, than the sum of their parts thus, from both the practical and cultural standpoint, any effort to divorce one from the other, diminishes the tradition as a whole.

I am blessed to have *learned* at the feet of the great matriarchs of my family and community, and it is to them that I dedicate this website and my ongoing devotion to '*the things we do*'.

The contents of this book are recorded oral history. Its purpose is to document this oral history and provide a road map for all spiritual seekers and lovers of tradition. May it guide you in reconnecting with your roots, and assist you in forging a tradition and legacy of your own.

S'a benedica,

Rue
West Kelowna, British Columbia, Canada

ITALY

Italy is a country republic in Europe characterized by its boot-shaped peninsula and two islands, one to the south, Sicily, and the other to the west, Sardinia. The capital of Italy is Rome, and the official language is Italian. Italy is composed of twenty regions. It has a long Mediterranean (ocean) coastline to the west and an Adriatic (ocean) coastline to the east. Italy as we know it today is a young country. Today's twenty regions of Italy became unified in 1861 by General Giuseppe Garibaldi. In 1946, the country of Italy was declared a republic.

People outside of Italy perceive it to be a homogenous country, but it is not. Each region has its own distinct language (dialect) and culture. Every city and small town within the region has its own dialect, customs, and tradition. I use the descriptor *Italian*, however, to be accurate; the Italian practices I write about in this book were more specifically brought over to North America by immigrants from the regions of Abruzzo, Campania, Puglia (Apulia), and Sicilia (Sicily).

Chapter 1

The Kitchen

The house I grew up in was typical of our neighborhood. There were two floors: the upstairs and the downstairs. The upstairs consisted of the main front entrance door, the living room we never used, bedrooms, bathrooms, and an immaculate, almost shrine-like kitchen that we also never used. We only spent time upstairs to bathe and sleep. Downstairs is where life happened. Most homes had what served as the real front door cut out of the main garage door. You entered through that door and walked through an immaculately kept garage. Sometimes, workspace was reserved for mothers who worked piecework contracts on industrial sewing machines from home.

For most Italian families, the garage was also the space used to can tomatoes and process all sorts of vegetables to store for the winter. It was also where we made wine. Typically, it had a sink, and some people even had an old stove that was still fully functional, plus a table and chairs. The garage was pretty much another kitchen. The importance of the kitchen is evident in the fact that the Italians of my hometown typically had THREE kitchens in their homes.

The kitchen has always been and continues to be the most important and sacred room of the house. In fact, my paternal ancestors called the kitchen *la camera de lu foche* (the room of the fire) because their kitchens always contained a hearth. I hope to one day have a kitchen hearth; in the meantime, I am content that I have a gas range.

The kitchen, my kitchen, is the room where nourishing meals are prepared. It is where afternoon coffee is brewed and stories shared. When someone doesn't feel well, it is where chicken soup simmers and herbal teas for any ailment are brewed. Stored in the cupboards are dishes and cups, some of which once graced my mother's kitchen. It is where my herbs, spices, and oils are stored. It is the room where old friends sit and enjoy a cookie with freshly brewed espresso and share their joys and sorrows. It's where I go to pray. I meditate while I clean and pray while I cook. It is the room where most of my memories live. It is my temple, shrine, and altar.

» When people come to see me for a card reading or spiritual/magical guidance, we sit at the kitchen table.

» When a member of my family is ill, I prepare remedies in my kitchen.

» Important family conversations are had at the kitchen table.

» When the energy in my home feels stagnant or when I or a member of my family feels unsettled, I go to work to clear the energies and bless my home, beginning with my kitchen.

» When I need to visit with my people who are dear to me, who have since departed this world, I do so in my kitchen.

» When I need guidance from my ancestors, I communicate with them from my kitchen.

» Blessing rituals are conducted in my kitchen.

» Magic and spell work are carried out in my kitchen.

» When my kitchen is in disorder, everything is in disorder.

» When my kitchen is in order, everything is in order.

» When I am feeling rattled or unfocused, the quickest and most effective way I know to center myself and regain focus is to put my kitchen in order.

From a practical viewpoint, my kitchen contains everything I need to practice my craft.

My dad would say, "The kitchen is the heart and soul of a house. No matter how big or small, it must be well maintained and cared for. It must contain the entire natural world. Otherwise, it is just a room to store food and cooking tools."

I have had many kitchens. I've moved quite a bit in my life, and I've both rented and owned. I've had old and outdated kitchens in desperate need of repair. I've had brand-new kitchens and everything in between. They were all the heart and soul of where I lived, house or apartment—except for one. The kitchen in the tiny two-room apartment I rented in college was just a room where I stored food and kitchen tools. It was the only one I didn't fill with the natural world, and it indeed made a difference.

The kitchen contains all four elements in its basic configuration:

Air: Refrigerator. Freezer. Range hood ventilation. If you're lucky, a window above the kitchen sink; if not, some kind of fan, ceiling, standing, etc. It gets hot and steamy in the kitchen, and Italians are fanatical about ventilation!

Earth: The stones in my water filter. Cast-iron pots and pans. Granite or marble mortar and pestle. Wooden spoons and bowls. Straw baskets. Clay pots.

Fire: Stove or range, oven, electrical cooking appliances.

I am partial to gas ranges. I think the reason is that my parents had a gas range when I was little. When I went to live with my aunt and uncle, they (and all my neighbors and other aunts and uncles) had hearths in their main living area! I also think it is because I am a Leo, a fire sign, and fire just makes me happy!

Water: Sink and faucet.

I also have a water filter on my kitchen counter. It's the kind with a ceramic disc filter and marbles and stones. It looks like a fish tank, but I don't have fish in it because fish would poop in there and that would defeat the whole water filter thing.

For the most part, I use the same supplies for magic that I use for cooking.

Continuing in the vein of bringing the natural world into the kitchen:

Herbs and Spices

Herbs and spices are all in their most natural form, fresh or dried. Whenever possible, grow your own, in your kitchen. Each plant has a spirit. The more spirits in your house, the more power resides there. I have a cupboard dedicated to dried herbs and spices. I love to cook, and therefore, my collection is quite diverse. Herbs and spices are used in cooking, medicine, and magic. The herbs (leaves, not ground) and spices (whole and ground) you must have on hand are the following:

Anise: It can be in the form of ground spice, star anise, or anisetta liqueur.

Basil: I grow my own, and I always have freeze-dried, dehydrated, and fresh on hand.

Bay laurel: I use whole leaves; freeze-dried when I can find it; otherwise, dehydrated.

Black pepper: Whole peppercorns.

Chamomile: Dried whole flowers and leaves.

Chili pepper: Fresh, dried whole, dried flakes. I have a treasured large glass jam jar filled with dried whole chili peppers from my late uncle Pellegrino's garden.

Cinnamon: Ground and sticks.

Coriander: Seeds and ground.

Cumin: Seeds and ground.

Mint/spearmint: I grow mint for fresh and dried leaves.

Oregano: I grow my own for fresh. I mainly use dried leaves. There are different kinds of oregano—my favorite being Sicilian and Greek oregano still on the stem.

Parsley: I grow my own when I can. Freeze-dried.

Rosemary: I grow my own. I also have a much-treasured eight-ounce glass jar of dried rosemary needles, one-third full, that my parents bought when they were newlyweds in 1958. The price sticker says seventy-five cents.

Rue: I grow it for fresh and dried leaves.

Sage: I grow my own for fresh and dried leaves.

Spikenard: Seeds, root.

Thyme: I grow my own for fresh and dried leaves.

This list is not exhaustive, but it provides you with a good start. I strongly urge you to raid your relatives' pantries, especially older relatives, and ask them to give you whatever they don't use—especially old herbs and spices. Don't believe the TV cooking gurus who tell you to toss your herbs and spices in the trash after three months. They last decades stored in little glass jars when protected from heat and moisture, and they are magical.

Some Basic Pantry Supplies

A well-stocked pantry is your magico-medicinal arsenal. Keep some basic supplies on hand, and you will be ready for everything. You can cook up a delicious meal or a little magic at a moment's notice.

Here's my list: garlic, onions, lemons, oranges, good olive oil, red wine vinegar, coarse sea salt, sun-dried tomatoes, dried porcini mushrooms, dried pasta, canned tomato paste, canned whole tomatoes, anchovies in oil, canned baby clams, rosewater, orange flower water, coffee beans, sugar, and honey.

Magic Tools

There's no need to go out and buy special Italian witchcraft tools.

The first reason is that they do not exist. The second and most important reason is that all the tools you need are already in your kitchen. All my cookware, dishes, utensils, glasses, cups—*everything* in my kitchen is used for cooking, natural medicine, and magic. However, no matter how modest, every item in my kitchen is carefully thought out and curated. Most of my kitchen equipment is inherited from my family and my husband's family. There is a lot of family history in my dish cupboard, for example.

I also peruse thrift stores for special vintage kitchen items. I collect only items that I can use. Over the years I have found—and I'm certain a number of you may relate with what I am going to say—that these items that are so special to me, they hold a tremendous amount of power. So much so, that if I attempt to cook something special in, say, a pot I never use or one I borrowed from someone else, not only does my food not turn out as good, but I've experienced the worst disasters. I won't take that chance with food. I definitely will never take that chance with magic!

Setting Up Your Kitchen

The first thing you need to do is set up your sacred space, your temple, your altar, your shrine. Are you ready?

This may be a big job, depending on the current state of your kitchen. I can't promise this task won't be work, but I promise it will be worthwhile, because once it's done, it will be a joy to have and to maintain. I recommend you do this when you know you have at least two days. You can enlist the help of family members and friends for the first part.

Part One

Remove everything from your kitchen that does not belong in a kitchen. If it is not used to cook, it doesn't belong there. I know, I know—you probably have tons of cupboard space, and you may not be using it all for kitchen purposes. So, you figured, why not use those cupboards to store sporting equipment, nail polish, all those magazines you're hanging onto that you may need some day. . . .

Now, move all your kitchen stuff to boxes or, if you have the space, another room. Empty your kitchen like you're moving out. Now do a deep cleaning of your kitchen. Scrub every nook and cranny clean from ceiling to floor. Everything inside and out. Clean out your fridge, and clean your stove as well as your oven. Remove anything hanging on the walls. Wash the walls, and if you can, give them a fresh coat of paint. If you have windows, wash the drapes and blinds, and clean the windows. Don't forget light fixtures and the one thing I hate the most: the range hood.

Once your kitchen is empty and scrubbed clean, you may want to order some pizza. Seriously, I know this is very hungry work, and you deserve a meal break!

Go through all your kitchen stuff. Keep what you love, discard what you never use and don't care for, and move it out of your house to discard or donate before continuing.

Now move the boxes of stuff you are keeping back into your kitchen. If you have things that need to be washed first, then do that. The next part of this process you need to do on your own because it takes some thought and because it must be *you* who sets it up.

Part Two

Stand in your kitchen. Feel that stillness? You did that merely by cleaning it. Turn on some background Italian music. Your kitchen needs to have flow. I keep all my herbs and spices in a cupboard near my stove. My glasses and coffee mugs near my coffee machine. My dishes in one cupboard. My pots and pans in another. The only items in my drawers are kitchen utensils and clean dish towels. All my dry goods are nicely organized in my pantry. The contents of my freezer and refrigerator are organized as well.

Once everything is put away where it belongs, stop. Do you feel that calm, still energy? You did that. This is the part of the exercise where you will begin to feel a connection to your kitchen. You have brought the natural world into your kitchen and that feeling is your kitchen's spirit(s).

Part Three

Now it's time to clear, bless, and ward your kitchen.

To clear or purify, simply toss a pinch of salt in every corner. Now sweep from the corners inward. Collect the salt and toss it out the back door.

In a two-quart pot, add three cinnamon sticks, three whole cloves, a teaspoon of sea salt, and a lemon cut in half. Fill the pot three-quarters of the way with water. Bring to a boil and then lower the heat and allow to simmer for one to two hours. This mixture smells amazing and clears not only your kitchen, but your entire home! Turn off the heat and leave to cool. Once it is cooled, remove the lemon and pour the rest in a clean spray bottle. I keep this purifying/

blessing solution on hand for whenever I need to clear the air, so to speak.

I purify my kitchen whenever it's feeling a little cluttered or the energy feels stagnant or stale.

The following amulets work well to ward your kitchen: garlic, dried whole peperoncino, coarse sea salt, a photo or statue of a patron saint or deity whose protection you wish to invoke, and a palm blessed on Palm Sunday. My Neapolitan relatives and friends simply kept a little bowl of sea salt on their kitchen counter. If they were business owners, they also kept a little bowl of sea salt on their store counter. My dad, who was born in Abruzzo, hung braided garlic and a string of dried peperoncino on his kitchen wall. A blessed, braided palm from Palm Sunday hung on the wall above the kitchen door. I've seen ceramic garlic and peperoncino on twine braids at the Italian grocery store in my town. As for me, I ward my kitchen with a San Giuseppe votive candle from Saint Joseph's Oratory in Montreal that has never been lit and has been with me since my very first apartment. I also have a tiny little diptych of Padre Pio (now San Pio), and there is always garlic and dried whole peperoncino present. On the wall above the entrance to my kitchen is a dried sprig of rue from one of my rue bushes.

Finally, you want to have some sort of talisman in your kitchen that represents abundance to you. It can be anything from a beautiful painting of a table set with fruit, vegetables, bread, wine, and cheese, to always keeping a tin of cookies on the counter. These paintings or prints used to be very common in Italian households, and a tin of cookies always comes in handy for those little afternoon coffee breaks!

The most important thing is to choose amulets and talismans that fit your personality and mean something to you.

Chapter 2

Sacred Spaces and Home Altars

Growing up Italian meant to be always surrounded by the outward expression of our culture and spirituality. We never spoke of home altars. The only "altar" we knew was in church. We didn't even have a name for these holy spaces that surrounded us indoors and outdoors. Although nameless, their presence was seen and felt everywhere.

In my Italian neighborhoods in Quebec and in Connecticut, Madonna statues graced impeccably tended front lawns surrounded by low, black wrought-iron fences. They were so common that I didn't pay any attention to them until the neighborhoods changed, and they began to disappear. Occasionally, a statue would be in disrepair and the yard a mess. This condition was extremely uncommon, and it usually meant that the person living at that home was ill or infirm and thus unable to care for the yard. It wouldn't remain in that sad state very long. There was always a neighbor ready and willing to give the Madonna statue a fresh lick of paint and plant some flowers. It was an act of service toward the person living in that home *and* to the Madonna. Tending to the aesthetics of the statue, mowing the lawn, and weeding the flowerbed were an offering, a prayer, with the intention to keep misfortune away from the home and family of both the person needing the yard tended to as well as the person doing the tending. A family in mourning would have a red memorial votive lit, and the flowers from the funeral would be placed there after the service. Children were never permitted to play in the front yard. They were also told to take care to not damage anyone's property and to be nice to each other because la Madonna is always watching. The front yard of a home was practically sacred ground.

These sacred spaces were everywhere in the homes and places of business and were as individual as the person who set them up, yet at the same time they followed a similar theme. The most common were, of course, statues of their family's patron saint. Inside the homes of many of my friends and relatives were tables or shelves with at least one statue of a saint. These tables or shelves were always meticulously clean and tidy. The statues were adorned with rosary beads that shimmered like diamonds, fresh flowers, silk flowers, sparkly ribbons, and colorful feathers and sometimes money. Beneath the statues were elaborately embroidered or crocheted doilies handmade years before when the matriarch was a young girl. Upon the doilies were offerings of fresh fruit, flowers, olive oil, coffee beans, and money. Most often these altars were illuminated day and night with candles, whether wax or electric. The most common statues found in homes were the Miraculous Madonna, the Immaculate Heart Madonna, the Sacred Heart of Jesus, and Our Lady of Lourdes. People who could not afford a statue hung a picture of their patron saint. Every family had their own patron saint. These patron saints were the patron saints of their Italian paese (village) of origin as well as any saint that may have granted them a miracle. Some were well known, such as Saint Anthony of Padua; others less known, such as Saint Eustace.

Widowed nonnas who lived with their children and grandchildren maintained a sacred space on a tall dresser in their tiny bedrooms. Upon these tall dressers were statues of their patron saints, photos of their ancestors, photos of any siblings and children who were deceased. Their wedding photo. The most recent wedding anniversary photo, and a large portrait of their deceased husband as a young man.

The nativity scene, manger, or crèche is also a home altar. It began to appear slowly on the first day of December, beginning with the landscape and angels, The three wise men at the furthest corner of the altar, then shepherds and their animals. On December 24, Mary and Joseph were added, and at midnight, Baby Jesus would arrive. The nativity scene would remain long after the Christmas tree was taken down on January 7. Around the end of January, it was packed up for another year to make room for the Madonna of la Candelora and the returning of the light on February 2. My favorite Madonna of la Candelora statue had a real functioning crown that fit candles all around her head. The most commonly found ones had light bulbs in the place of candle flames.

Saint Joseph Altar

Saint Joseph is the husband of the Virgin Mary and foster father to Jesus. He is a very important saint and patron to Italian families.

There is no custom as telling about my ancestors' relationship to their saints as the Saint Joseph altar. Let me explain.

The Saint Joseph altars of my family's regions were smaller and simpler than the opulent, elaborate Saint Joseph altars originating from Sicily that evolved into the spectacle of the Saint Joseph altars of North America and, notably, New Orleans. The Saint Joseph altars of New Orleans are beautiful examples of how a custom brought over by Sicilian immigrants evolved into its own distinct thing. The feast day of Saint Joseph is March 19, and it always occurs during Lent. Therefore, my family's Saint Joseph altars were much more low-key, so to speak, and the offerings were Lenten food offerings (foods not containing meat, poultry, eggs, and dairy). Citrus fruit, fish, a bowl of *minestra di bietola e patate* (chard and potato soup), dried fava beans, *biscotti secchi* (dry, twice-baked cookies prepared without fat), almonds, hazelnuts, walnuts, wine, liquor, and *zeppole*. The zeppole of my tradition, and there are two varieties, are made of an unsweetened fried dough, like a donut, and dusted with a touch of powdered sugar.

Although they are cooked in oil, there is no fat in the dough, and it contains just enough sugar to help feed the yeast for leavening. The other type of zeppole is a cream puff made of choux pastry and filled with a (not so Lenten) custard made with eggs, milk, small amounts of sugar, some flour for thickening, and a thick strip of fresh lemon peel for aroma. Atop the cream is a dab of *amarena* (bitter) cherries preserve. I love the symbolism of the cream puff zeppole. The amarena preserve is there to symbolize that in life we have to always be prepared to take the bitter with the sweet.

The feast of Saint Joseph and the altar are not a request for Saint Joseph to bless the family with abundance. They are payment for abundance already rendered the previous year:

> »   If a family had a bad year, then Saint Joseph may have a small altar, or none at all.

> »   If the family enjoyed a prosperous year, then Saint Joseph's altar reflects that.

To put it simply, the size of the Saint Joseph altar is commensurate with how happy the family was with him based on whether they had had an abundant harvest and prosperous year. Now, I know what you are thinking. At first glance, it seemed logical to me too that, of course, the altar would be smaller or nonexistent if they had a bad year. They wouldn't have anything to place on the altar. Conversely, of course, they would set a more elaborate altar if they had a good year, because their pantry was stocked. This, although the logical conclusion, is not the reasoning.

The Italian ancestors' relationship with their saints was the complete opposite of their relationship with the Trinity (God, Jesus, and the Holy Ghost) and Mother Mary. Our ancestors served and feared God, Jesus, the Holy Ghost, and la Madonna. They viewed the saints, however, in the same way they viewed the old gods—as serving them. Therefore, if they petitioned a saint, and the saint didn't grant them what they asked for, they threatened to withdraw their love and devotion by turning their attention away and to a different saint. This practice of "saint punishing" will be explored further in chapter 13.

Our homes also had spiritual spaces and imagery other than Roman Catholic. Angel statues and pictures were everywhere. Marble, cement, or painted plaster statues of old Roman gods, such as Bacchus (god of wine), Cupid (god of love), Diana (goddess of the hunt), Mercury (god of commerce and the arts), and Venus (goddess of beauty and fertility), to name the more common ones, graced the front lawn, backyard, or entrance way of quite a few of the homes of my relatives and friends. Figurines or statues of certain animals such as bears, lions, eagles, falcons, wild horses, wolves, dogs, sows, panthers, turtles, toads, and deer were in the home, the front yard, and the backyard. They weren't just decoration, though; they were representations of the deities and animal spirits whose influence and protection we intended to invoke.

Years went on, and the first generation to immigrate to North America retired or died. Their kids, born in North America, began taking over or selling their parents' homes. Suddenly, the icons of my childhood were seen as tacky and outdated. These gods and animal statues were a major part of the landscape of my childhood. Now that they are gone, it seems the gods and spirits have also gone.

Home altars are not limited to just saints, nor are you limited to having just one. I have two altars just in my home office.

So, let's look at the types of altars and ideas of how to set them up.

Ancestral Altar

Placement

As with real estate, the most important part of setting up your altar is location. For your ancestral altar, pick a part of your home that feels central. Choose an area that has a lot of activity. A family room, an entranceway, a main corridor, a corner of the dining area—all are areas of your home that are excellent places for an ancestral altar. What is important is that the location feels right to you.

Surface

The surface you choose depends highly on the space you have and what you wish to display. If you have many photographs of your ancestors, you may want to dedicate a wall to them. They can be arranged in many ways. You can arrange the photographs in the shape of a tree or a circle with your oldest ancestors at the top and your youngest, more recent ancestors at the bottom. Deceased ancestors such as grandparents, great-grandparents, great-great-grandparents, and so on are placed at the top (heaven, afterlife); and more recent ancestors and living parents and grandparents, toward the bottom (earth). You will want to arrange them in a shape other than square or rectangular so that it suggests continuation. Continuation into the past beyond your earliest ancestors is represented by leaving room between the top of their photographs and the ceiling. Continuation into the future beyond you and/or your living descendants is represented by leaving room below their photographs. I've witnessed a zia (aunt) physically move furniture around at another zia's house because "that furniture against the wall, under the photographs blocks grandchildren from being born." This is one example of many ways to set up your ancestral altar.

Another configuration is to have only deceased ancestor photographs displayed on a dedicated shelf or table with personal effects such as their eyeglasses. Other examples of objects for your ancestral altar are those representing their region or town of origin, their occupations, their crafts, and so on. For instance, my paternal ancestors were artisans, specifically sculptors originating from Puglia and Abruzzo. In this example, I would place the photographs I have of my late father, his brother, his father, his uncles, and his grandfather on a shelf with, say, a hammer and chisel that I inherited from my father.

Your ancestral altar can be expanded to include objects like in my hammer and chisel example, or sacramental objects such as saint medals. My father's favorite saints were Padre Pio, Saint Francis of Assisi, and Saint Michael Archangel. Because my father also had a strong connection to the natural world, I may choose to surround him with religious figures or beautiful stones and animals.

What if you didn't inherit a box of photographs? What if you don't know who your ancestors were? We all come from somewhere and feel the pull of wherever that somewhere may be. Suppose all you are able to discover is that your mother's mother may have been from Venice, for example. Read up on the history of Venice. Learn about the Venice your grandmother may have lived in. Find a picture of Venice that moves you. Hang it on your wall. Meditate on it and let your imagination paint you a mental picture of who your maternal grandmother was and what life may have been like for her. The photo doesn't have to be of the correct house or even the correct location. All that matters is that you start somewhere.

The purpose of this altar is more than just a place to honor your ancestors. Although they are deceased, our ancestors do take interest in our day-to-day goings-on. They are present through good times, like when we are celebrating our successes. They are present through hard times, to comfort us during times of conflict and uncertainty. Positioning this altar in a central part of your home includes them in events of daily life. I like the dining area the best because the dining table is where we come together as a family and where celebrations take place. This altar also provides us with a physical place to meet with them to seek counsel and comfort when we need it. The belief is that they see all from their centrally located vantage point, and therefore, when we need counsel or comfort, we don't even have to explain what has transpired. They know because they are nearby.

Saint or Deity Altar

Placement

The placement of a saint or deity altar depends on many factors. The first factor is whether you feel comfortable with your saints or deities being displayed where everyone who comes to your home can see them. You have to also take into consideration who you share your home with and their feelings about a saint or deity altar. I have been to homes where the saint altar is right in the front entrance facing outward. It is the first thing you'll see when you open the front door. You may find this placement comforting, or maybe this does not appeal to you, or maybe you don't want your altar where everyone can see it. Use your judgment and do what feels right.

Surface

The surface for this altar can be a wall, shelf, or table. You can have an altar dedicated to one saint or deity, or you can have a group of saints on one altar and your deities on another. You can also have a combination of saints and deities.

Statues are not always easy to find and, when you do find them, they can be prohibitively expensive. Don't be discouraged. You don't need to spend a fortune to create a beautiful altar. I am constantly checking out consignment shops, thrift stores, and garage sales for statues or symbolic objects for my altar. Dollar stores and department stores also sometimes have just the right thing. I was over the moon when I found a novena candle, the kind sold in Latin bodegas, of Saint Barbara at the dollar store. Over the moon because it is so rare to find anything of the sort where I live. I found the image of Saint Joseph I like the best on the Internet. I printed it in grayscale on plain eight-by-eleven-inch printer paper because I didn't own a color printer at the time, and I framed it in a wood frame I purchased at the dollar store. This portrait of Saint Joe has been the focal point of my altar for nearly twenty years.

The belief is that this altar is a physical door or window to the spiritual world. It is the window where we seek out our saints and deities to request their help and is the door they use to enter our home and our lives.

Other Types of Altars

While all works of medicine and magic were typically performed at the kitchen table, counter, and on the stove, works of blessing were most commonly done at the feet of saint statues or before portraits of saints. Your working altar is wherever you choose to perform your works of medicine and magic. Whether it is your kitchen table, a small table in front of a window, or a flat slab of rock in your backyard, this surface is sacred even when you aren't using it for magic. Don't allow it to become cluttered. Wipe it down to clean it physically and energetically before each use, and never, ever, place your feet on it. That includes shoes. This especially applies to the dinner table and kitchen counter and altar, but also extends to any table surface in your home. Why, you ask? It's an Italian thing. I was taught that angels live on the table and to place something as dirty as a shoe on the table is sacrilege. Shoes and the soles of their feet are what Saint Michael Archangel and Our Lady Queen of Heaven use to crush the devil/serpent.

The supper table is a working altar at all times. The surface should always be clean and tidy. It should never be cluttered with junk mail and dirty dishes. Always set the table for meals. Whether you are enjoying a meal on your own or with twenty people, take the time to make it inviting. After the meal, wipe the table clean and push all the chairs in. Begin by taking care of your supper table, and you will see an immediate improvement in your family life. If you live alone and you are lonely, you will suddenly have company to share your meals. Years ago, when I saw clients in my home for tarot readings, I would decide whether I was open for business or not by how I set my kitchen table. On days when I wanted to see clients, I would wipe my table down after breakfast and place my tarot deck and a lit candle where I normally sat. The chair where clients sat would be pulled out to welcome them. More often than not, a client would phone wanting a reading within the hour. Some of those days turned into back-to-back appointments. On days when I was not available, I would wipe my table down after breakfast and push all the chairs in. My tarot deck and candle would be stored away. No one phoned for an appointment on those days.

Your altars can be as elaborate and as ornate as you like them to be. If you are a more private person, you may choose a very simple and minimally adorned altar. The items on your altar are outward, physical manifestations of your inner spirituality. If you work mainly with elemental spirits, your altar may be as simple (and powerful) as displaying symbols of the four elements on your mantle. My Zia Rosella was really big on decorating her saint altar for the season. At Christmas, Padre Pio wore a red-and-white Santa Claus hat on his head and a little festive scarf around his neck. In the spring, my zia would bring out the little chicks and bunnies and silk daffodils.

The only thing that is nonnegotiable is to keep your altar tidy and clean. Tidiness and cleanliness are of high importance in Italian culture. Cleanliness is medicine. Cleanliness is prayer. Cleanliness is magic. No matter how extravagant or humble your altar is, all that matters is that you keep it tidy, clean, and all the objects in good repair. If you drop your little statue of Saint Michael Archangel and his arm breaks off, carefully repair it immediately. The principle of devotion demonstrated with physical care applies to your altars as it does in the example I gave at the beginning of this chapter with tending the garden surrounding the Madonna in the front yard.

You can choose to have separate altars for saints and deities. Personally, I like all the saints, deities, and animal and earth spirits whom I have a working relationship with housed on the same altar. They are my spiritual multidisciplinary team. Crosses, saint prayer cards, corni (plural of corno, an amulet in the shape of a bull's horn typically made of red coral or plastic) censers, candles, and tarocchi (tarot) are among the items I bring together. My spirituality is informed by my past with respect to my culture and tradition and evolved from my personal experience. My view is that prayer and works of magic are two sides of the same coin. Therefore, there is no conflict between the sacred and the profane.

Setting Up Your Altar

I follow the exact same principles for setting up my altar as for setting up my kitchen:

1. Declutter the room where your altar will be located. Pay specific attention to the surface that will house your altar, as well as the area surrounding it. Thoroughly clean the room. Clear the energy and bless the space.

2. Using a clean, damp cloth, wipe all the objects that you will be placing on your altar. This removes visible dust, removes stagnant energy, and places your personal energy onto the objects. You will actually feel the objects refreshed and renewed when you do this.

3. Place your statue(s) or photo(s) on your altar.

4. Now add elements of the natural world. Stones, feathers, animal figures and photos, and plants are some of the items on my altar. My dogs always instinctively gravitate to resting beside my altar. This tells me there is natural energy present. The natural energy in them is attracted to the natural energy of my altar.

5. Now add elements that resonate with you on a practical level. A cast-iron cauldron, pentacle candleholder, and a wand I made from a fallen willow tree branch are some of the items that resonate with my practice and are therefore placed on my altar.

6. Place offerings to your saint/deity. Fresh flowers, cake, fruit, and brandy are some of the offerings I place on my altar.

7. The last thing I do is light a brand-new candle and burn some incense on the altar.

When my altar becomes dusty or the energy in my home feels stagnant, I declutter, clean, and reset my altar. The same applies before conducting any work of magic.

Chapter 3

Food

*T*his chapter is dedicated to recipes because food is where it all began and food is everything. Food brings people together. Food honors our ancestors and the region a family hails from. No matter how rich or how poor the family, Italian food is good food.

» Food is medicine when we prepare a meal for someone who is ill.

» Food is magic when we prepare a meal for someone who is the object of our desire.

» Food is love when we cook for our families.

» Food is comfort. Food brings us back to ourselves by reconnecting us to our ancestors.

Food is inevitably the most discussed subject on any Italian witchcraft forum I have ever participated in. The most common emails I receive begin like this: "Dear Rue, I saw your website and was hoping you can help me. My grandmother passed away when I was young, but I can still remember this soup she used to make for me when I visited her on Saturdays. Can you help me figure out what it was so I can make it?"

The Magic in Food

"I can taste the love."

"The secret ingredient is love."

"Food is love."

"The way to a man's heart is through his stomach."

Love is not a physical ingredient. Love is an emotion. Love is an abstract concept. Cooking is alchemy, and intention is the element that transforms into love in the finished dish. Food is always handled with extreme care. From the cheapest, toughest cut to an expensive cut of Kobe beef, it is all handled with the same degree of gratitude, respect, and reverence.

What does it mean to "handle" the food with respect? It means just that. We place the food carefully into a pan or pot. We praise it. Praising the raw ingredients always results in a successful dish. We praise the raw ingredients when they are beautiful, such as the perfectly round tomato or the perfectly flawless lemon rind. When working with less perfect or downright ugly ingredients such as a utility chicken that may be missing a leg or a wing, we joke about it and give it more love.

We cook with our hands. Our clean, bare hands touch every single ingredient. We massage the roast with a rub made of olive oil and spices. We season by literally adding a pinch of salt and pepper in benediction. We talk to our food. Of course, for some foods we prepare, it isn't appropriate or practical to handle with our hands, such as when preparing a cake batter. In this case, once the batter is in the pan, we kiss our fingertips and touch them to the pan before placing it in the oven.

Traditional Recipes

All the recipes in this chapter are from real people. I collected the bulk of these recipes from people who brought their food customs from their hometown in Italy to North America and had to adapt to the ingredients found here. Other recipes were collected in Italy. Many of these recipes are basic and pretty much accessible anywhere in cookbooks and on the Internet. Others may be unique and even obscure. I hope they delight you as much as they delight me.

A few words about ingredients: in keeping with tradition, ingredients must be of the best quality your budget will allow and always closest to how they are found in nature. This concept is expressed in the Italian word *genuina*. Genuina means the genuine article, unprocessed, pure, the way Mother Nature created it. Italian food means wholesome ingredients prepared simply and combined in balance. There's only one thing I need to warn you about: Italians don't really follow or give out recipes. Instructions go something like this: "Take a good, fresh chicken, massage it nicely with a handful of herbs, oil the pan, place the chicken in it, make sure you lay the chicken on its back because laying the chicken facedown is disrespectful to the animal that sacrificed its life and will bring serious illness to the family, and pour some olive oil, you know, as much as it needs, measure it by eye, and place it in a hot oven, cook until cooked."

I will do my best to give you basic recipes. Then it is up to you to customize them and make them your own. Who knows? Maybe you will find a long-lost recipe in this collection. Maybe you will find a recipe for a dish you have completely forgotten but your nonna made all the time. Food brings people together. Food is the tie that binds us to our ancestors.

To simplify things, I will use the days of the week as a guide.

Saturday

As I mentioned at the start of this book, Saturday was and still is my favorite day of the week. It is the day of housekeeping, laundry, and grocery shopping. A very busy day, it only makes sense that meals consist of foods that, for the most part, make themselves. The family fends for itself for breakfast and lunch and then comes together for supper. One example of a traditional Saturday supper is brodo and pizza.

Brodo (Broth)

The humblest ingredients can create the richest broth, provided you don't rush it. Brodo is started at dawn and simmers ever so gently all day until suppertime, which on Saturdays is anywhere between five and seven in the evening.

Brodo is believed to have magical healing powers. I cannot even count how many stories I have been told. They all begin with someone close to death or with an incurable disease that even the doctor's medicine couldn't cure. They all end with "after so many days/weeks/ months of drinking brodo every day, they were cured." Whatever the ailment, brodo is the medicine. Brodo is also a valuable nutritional supplement when food is scarce. No matter how poor a family was, they could always afford bones to make brodo. I can't help but chuckle now when I see all the current articles on the virtues of "bone broth." I can hear all my ancestors exclaiming in a derisive "Pensano che hanno scoperta l'america" ("They think 'they' discovered America"), and then exploding in hysterical laughter.

Brodo di Gallina/Pollo (Hen/Chicken Broth)

There is an Italian saying: "gallina vecchia fa buon brodo" ("an old hen makes good broth"). It means age brings experience and wisdom. If you can't get an old hen, a chicken will do just fine.

Ingredients

    1 roasting chicken or stewing hen

    4 large carrots

    4 ribs celery

    2 medium yellow onions (remove outer skin and slice off the
        root end)

    6 cloves garlic

    4 fresh bay leaves (dry is okay, as long as the leaves are intact)

    12 whole peppercorns

    ½ cup dry pastina for every quart of broth

1. First, place your chicken into a stockpot large enough to
    accommodate your chicken lying down on its back, and then
    add all the other ingredients.

2. Fill the pot with cold water, leaving about three inches of
    room at the top.

3. Turn the heat on medium/low. If the water comes to a boil,
    turn down the heat until it is a gentle simmer. Carefully skim
    the foam off the top.

4. Simmer for at least eight hours, adding water as the broth
    cooks down.

5. Carefully remove the chicken, vegetables, and aromatics
    from the broth.

6. Strain the broth through a fine mesh sieve and then bring it
    to a boil in a clean pot.

7. Add half a cup of dry pastina (tiny pasta in the shape of stars
    or alphabets) for every quart of broth.

8. Once the pastina is cooked, turn off the heat and season the soup with salt to taste.

9. Place the lid on the pot and allow it rest a good fifteen to twenty minutes before serving.

10. Remove the chicken meat from the bones and skin and place them together with the vegetables on a serving dish. Season with a drizzle of good olive oil and salt and pepper to taste.

Pizza: Dough and Divination

Pizza dough is the simplest thing to prepare. Don't let this simplicity fool you. Preparing pizza dough is also a form of divination. My Neapolitan aunts were almost obsessive when it came to the meaning of the behavior of the pizza dough. For them, any deviation from how it was supposed to behave meant that evil forces were to blame. (It could also mean that your flour or yeast is stale.) Provided you are using fresh ingredients, your results should be consistent. Here are some examples of things that can go wrong and what my zie divined to be the reasons:

» If your dough doesn't rise: malocchio (the evil eye) is present. Someone is complimenting you behind your back, or they are thinking of you with envy in their hearts.

» If your dough rises correctly but then won't stretch out, instead snapping back like an elastic: an outcome you have been expecting will not turn out in your favor. There is resistance.

» If your dough rises correctly but breaks apart when you try to stretch it out: this indicates a health scare or is a sign that you need to take better care of yourself.

» If your dough rises too quickly, overproofs, and collapses: this indicates stress, anger, discord, distrust, betrayal, infidelity, or bankruptcy.

Pizza Dough

This recipe makes four nine- to ten-inch pizzas.

Ingredients

I envelope dried yeast (2½ teaspoons)

1½ cups warm water

½ teaspoon sugar

4 cups unbleached all-purpose flour

I teaspoon salt

1. Add the dried yeast, ½ cup of flour, and the sugar to the warm water.

2. Stir until mixed and then let it stand in a warm place until it becomes all foamy and doubles in volume.

3. On a clean board or counter, place the flour with the salt mixed in and make a well in the center.

4. Pour in your leavening mixture.

5. With your fingertips, stir the center while incorporating the flour. Do this until most of the flour is incorporated and you have a nice sticky ball of dough.

6. Spread out the remaining flour and place your dough ball onto it. Knead the dough with the heels of your hands until it is smooth and elastic.

7. Oil a large bowl and place the dough in it.

8. Cover the dough with a clean dish towel and place the bowl in a warm place where there aren't any drafts. Let the dough rise for one to two hours or until it doubles in size.

9. Once it has doubled in size, make a fist and punch down the dough and divide into four parts.

10. Roll each part into a ball and cover with the dish towel and leave to rise a second time. Let the dough rest for about an hour or until it has doubled in volume.

Now you are ready to make your pizzas.

1. Preheat your oven to 475 degrees Fahrenheit.

2. To form the pizzas, take a ball of dough and flatten the center with the heel of your hand and fingertips.

3. Spin the dough around on a lightly floured surface as you work to flatten the dough. The dough will stretch out, and a ridge will form around the edges.

My favorite pizza is La Marinara. The topping consists of Italian peeled tomatoes straight from the can and crushed by squeezing the whole tomatoes with clean hands until they take on a chopped appearance, a drizzle of olive oil, and some torn fresh basil leaves. Leave as is for La Marinara or top with your favorite toppings.

4. Bake your pizzas on the lowest rack of the oven for ten to fifteen minutes. Check your pizza at ten minutes to avoid burning it.

Sunday

No aroma transcends time and space uniting us with our ancestors more than the fragrance of onion frying in olive oil and tomato sauce simmering on Sunday morning. Every matriarch (and patriarch) had a signature sauce recipe. Every family had a different name for it based on their region and/or the specific contents in the pot. Plain tomato sauce without meat, we called "sauce" or "sugo"; and tomato sauce containing meat, we called "gravy" or "ragù." Sauce, sugo, ragù, gravy—we may never all agree on what to call it, but we can all agree that it is what coming home tastes like. Below is my late mother's recipe.

Sunday Gravy

Serves four to six people.

What You Will Need

> 1 25-ounce can of Italian peeled tomatoes to every one pound of meat.

> A stainless steel or enameled cast-iron pot large enough to hold the volume of gravy you are making.

Ingredients

1 onion

Olive oil (not extra virgin; just plain olive oil)

1 pound meat of your choice (choose one or a combination of: lamb belly; pork sausage; meatballs made with a combination of ground pork, beef, and veal)

1 25-ounce can Italian tomatoes

6 ounces water

Salt and pepper to taste

1. In a heavy pot, drizzle enough olive oil to cover the bottom.

2. Cut an onion in half and fry it in the oil on medium heat until the edges are browned. Remove the onion.

3. Brown the meat in the pot and then remove and reserve it on a plate.

4. Pour the tomatoes and the water into the pot. When this comes up to a simmer, return the meat to the pot, as well as the juices that drained onto the plate.

5. Stir to combine and cook uncovered low and slow for two hours or until the gravy tastes cooked.

6. Make sure to keep on eye on your gravy and stir it every half hour to make sure it isn't sticking on the bottom of your pot. If your gravy is reducing too much, add a little water no later than the last half hour.

7. Once the gravy is cooked, cook one package (one pound) of your favorite maccheroni (pasta). Penne goes perfectly with this gravy. Cook your pasta according to the instructions on the package. Drain and place in a serving bowl with half a stick of butter and one ladle of gravy on the bottom. Toss the maccheroni until coated. Add more gravy and toss until all the maccheroni are coated. This recipe makes just enough gravy to coat one pound of maccheroni.

8. Place the meat on a serving dish.

9. Toss some romaine lettuce in a light dressing of olive oil and red wine vinegar, thinly sliced red onion, salt, and pepper.

10. Don't forget the grated Parmiggiano and fresh, crusty, Italian bread for mopping up that gravy!

Monday

Minestra di verdure is basically a vegetable soup, but not the vegetable soup you may think it is. Minestra di verdure is a mix of greens, a legume, and a starch. We ate this soup four to five nights per week when I was a kid. It is easy to make, economical, and nourishing. Chard grew easily and abundantly in our backyard gardens. In the winter, our grocer had it. Everyone seemed to have bags of shelled Romano beans in their freezer. In a pinch, canned Romano beans work just as well. Minestra di verdure was considered an integral part of our diet. It served as an inexpensive and effective nutritional supplement. It was medicine for intestinal problems. It was believed that eating minestra di verdure cured and prevented *i vermi* (worms). These "worms" were perceived as both physical and metaphysical, the line between the two blurred so that they were one and the same. Indigestion and consti-pation would be attributed to i vermi. The cure was to eat minestra di verdure. Symptoms of depression, such as fatigue and withdrawal, were also attributed to i vermi. The cure was minestra di verdure. I guess the point is that minestra was good for you, so eat it!

Minestra di verdure

Ingredients

Olive oil

1 yellow onion, chopped fine

1 clove garlic, minced

1 teaspoon hot red chili flakes

1 bunch chard, chopped into bite-sized pieces, rinsed, and drained

1 potato, peeled, cubed, rinsed, and drained

1 19-ounce can Romano beans, rinsed and drained

2 quarts water

Salt and pepper to taste

1. Add a drizzle of olive oil to a soup pot, enough to completely cover the bottom.

2. Begin to warm the oil over medium heat.

3. Add the onion, garlic, and chili flakes to the pot. Cook until the onion looks soft.

4. Stir with a wooden spoon and don't take your attention away from it because it will burn. (If you burn the garlic or the chili flakes, start over from the beginning with fresh ingredients.)

5. Now add the water, cover, and bring to a boil.

6. Once your water is boiling, add the chard and the potato. Cook on medium-high heat for twenty minutes.

7. Add the Romano beans, turn down the heat to a simmer, and cook another twenty minutes.

8. Season your minestra with salt and pepper. Taste it in order to prevent over- or underseasoning.

9. Put on the lid and turn off the heat. Leave it to rest twenty minutes before serving to allow all the flavors to marry.

I love a sprinkling of Romano cheese on my minestra. Serve with crusty bread and leftover meat from Sunday. If you don't have any leftover meat, serve with a platter of cold cuts and cheese. If you have leftover soup, store in the refrigerator for a quick lunch tomorrow. It tastes even better the next day.

Tuesday

It so happens that it is a Tuesday as I am writing this, and *Pollo con patate al rosmarino* (rosemary chicken and potatoes) is what I am cooking for supper. This dish is the epitome of comfort food. Not only does this combination taste amazing, but it has medicine and magic in it. You can have a terrible, stressful day, but come suppertime, the aroma of this baking in your oven will soothe your mind and uplift your spirits. Our ancestors knew what they were doing when they combined these components. Chicken and potatoes are comforting foods that are easy to digest and always recommended when someone is feeling unsettled. Rosemary is a purifier and a ward against those evil spirits that like to toy with humans by giving them obsessive thoughts about impending doom, insomnia, sleepwalking, and recurring nightmares. Rosemary essential oil has antidepressant properties.

Pollo con patate al rosmarino
(Rosemary Chicken and Potatoes)

Serves four to six.

Ingredients

8 pieces chicken with bone in and skin on

4 russet potatoes, peeled, quartered, and rinsed

Olive oil

1 teaspoon fresh or dried rosemary (½ teaspoon if using ground)

Salt and pepper to taste

1. Preheat oven to 400 degrees Fahrenheit.

2. Place the chicken and potatoes in a large bowl.

3. Drizzle in some good olive oil and then, with clean hands, mix it all up so that each piece of chicken and potato is lightly coated in oil.

4. Sprinkle in the rosemary, salt, and pepper. Mix it all up again to make sure every piece of chicken and potato is seasoned.

5. Place it all in a greased roasting pan. Bake in the oven for forty to fifty minutes.

Wednesday

"Wednesday is Prince spaghetti day."

If you are my age or older, you'll remember this tag line from the TV commercial. If not, you can see it right now by typing the tagline into the YouTube search box. Tradition or brilliant marketing? I say it's a bit of both. I have relatives in the North End of Boston's traditionally Italian neighborhood where that commercial takes place. I didn't grow up there, and yet we too ate spaghetti on Wednesdays.

If you made a lot of Sunday gravy and set some aside in the fridge or freezer, well, today is the day to break it out. Reheat your sauce. Cook your spaghetti and enjoy.

I must confess that spaghetti is my favorite pasta. Here is one recipe that always brings me way back to carefree and simpler times.

Spaghetti al burro *(Spaghetti with Butter)*

Serves four to six.

Ingredients

1-pound package spaghetti

2 sticks (½ pound) butter, quartered

1 cup grated Parmiggiano Reggiano or Parmiggiano Padano cheese

1. Cook your spaghetti as per the instructions on the package.

2. When it is cooked, drain your spaghetti, making sure to reserve a half cup of the spaghetti water.

3. Place your butter in a big pasta serving bowl and then pour the hot spaghetti water over it, followed by the spaghetti.

4. With a large fork, carefully swirl your spaghetti around to coat it with the butter.

5. Now sprinkle the cheese over the entire surface of your spaghetti and swirl it some more to coat every strand with cheese.

Thursday

Back in the days before direct deposit and 24/7 supermarkets, Thursday was payday and grocery shopping day. This meant there was fresh bread, cold cuts, and cheese in the house! When my dad would say he ate a "sangweech" (sandwich), this is what he meant:

Sangweech (*Sandwich*)

Take a thick slice of crusty Italian bread. Drizzle some good olive oil on it. Layer on some thinly sliced prosciutto and a slice or two of provolone.

Or, for a more robust taste sensation, try thinly sliced soppressata Calabrese (spicy!) and pecorino Crotonese.

Tomato slices and any kind of pickled vegetable in oil and olives make an excellent accompaniment to the sangweech.

Friday

There was a time in my childhood when on Friday evenings, the waft of sardines frying filled the air of my neighborhood, which was densely populated with southern Italian immigrants. But this is not a fish recipe. Instead, I have selected a comfort dish very close to my heart, *carciofi* [pronounced CAR-cho-fee] (artichokes). Again, Italians believe preparing and eating certain foods is magic. Cook and eat *carciofi*, which have hearts in them, if you want to attract a love relationship. A word of caution though: always cook an even number of artichokes because they must be paired. Cooking an odd number will bring bad luck in love.

Carciofi (*Braised Artichokes*)

Serves four.

Ingredients

   4 artichokes, stems cut off, chokes removed, and leaves
      pried open

   Bread crumbs (homemade or store-bought)

   Garlic

Fresh Italian parsley

Olive oil

Salt and pepper

Polenta

1. Soak artichokes for thirty minutes in cold water and some lemon juice.

2. While your artichokes are soaking, take about a cup of bread crumbs and add to it two minced garlic cloves, ¼ cup of minced parsley, salt, and pepper.

3. Stir the dry mixture and add a bit of olive oil to moisten it so that you can pick it up with your fingertips.

4. Shake the excess water out of your artichokes and stuff the nooks and crannies of each one with your bread crumb mixture.

5. Drizzle enough olive oil to cover the bottom of a Dutch oven, preferably one just large enough to fit your artichokes sitting on their stem side.

6. Place your artichokes in the pot, drizzle a little olive oil over the top of your artichokes, and season with salt and pepper.

7. Boil some water in a kettle and add enough to the Dutch oven to reach roughly three-fourths of the height of your artichokes. Don't pour the water directly onto your artichokes; it will wash away your bread crumbs.

8. Cover the Dutch oven and braise on medium-low for one hour or until your artichokes are fork tender.

Serve with polenta prepared as per the instructions on the package. Don't forget to collect that beautiful sauce from the artichokes and drizzle it on your polenta.

Dolci *(Sweets)*

I always look forward to afternoon coffee. Coffee is customarily the black or espresso variety, drunk unsweetened and accompanied by a little taste of something sweet. This coffee ritual never fails to center me. It also allows me to stop for a moment and ponder that, in life, we must take the bitter (coffee) with the sweet (cookie).

Ciambella al gusto di limone
(Lemon-Flavored Donut-Shaped Cake)

Ciambella is my favorite dessert, breakfast, any-time cake. It resembles pound cake except that it contains more eggs.

Ingredients

> 6 large eggs
>
> 1 cup sugar
>
> Zest and juice of 1 lemon
>
> 6 ounces vegetable oil
>
> Pinch of salt
>
> 2 cups all-purpose flour
>
> 4 teaspoons baking powder

1. Preheat oven to 350 degrees Fahrenheit.

2. With an electric mixer, beat the eggs and sugar together until foamy.

3. Wash your lemon well and dry it thoroughly.

4. Grate the zest into the cake batter and then cut and squeeze the lemon using a juicer. Strain the juice and add to the mixing bowl.

5. Mix until blended.

6. Add vegetable oil. Mix until blended.

7. Add a pinch of salt and gradually add flour and baking powder and mix well until all the flour is incorporated and the batter is creamy.

8. Pour the batter into a greased angel food cake tin.

9. Bake for thirty-five to forty minutes or until the cake is golden and a skewer inserted comes out clean.

10. Run a plastic knife around the outer and inner portion of the cake to loosen it from the cake pan.

11. Remove and cool it completely on a baking rack.

12. Once the cake is completely cooled, store your ciambella in an airtight container at room temperature. If you can wait, it tastes better the day after you bake it, and it continues to taste great for up to four days.

Holidays (Feste)

Years ago, when my children were little, I got it in my head that I wanted to re-create the seafood supper my family customarily prepared on Christmas Eve. My husband and I together with two little girls in tow headed out to the nearest fish market. I picked out a variety of fish—seven to be exact. Once home, I began to prepare the Feast of the Seven Fishes. Oh, yeah, about that. This "Feast of Seven Fishes" is totally Italian American and completely unheard of in Italy by this name. Our Italian relatives did prepare a seafood supper for *La Vigilia* (Christmas Eve), however not the outrageous quantity we did in Canada and the United States.

Like I was saying, we brought all the fish home, and I began to prepare it. It had been almost twenty years since I last assisted in the preparation of these dishes. As I began to prep and cook, I invited all my closest ancestors to help me. The rest of the preparation is a blur. I watched in amazement as my hands re-created and surpassed the seafood dishes of my childhood. Time seemed to stand still, and everything came together beautifully. Effortlessly. My execution of the Feast of the Seven Fishes was in every way flawless. I felt both pride and awe at what I had accomplished on my own on my very first try. This year, La Vigilia was going to be perfectly traditional!

The table was set. My little girls and my husband helped me bring the food to the table. We sat down, and suddenly it all went terribly wrong. My girls, who never refused to eat anything, now refused to eat. They both began to cry. I was suddenly anxious and upset. I even felt an odd, disconnected anger. My husband was confused. He was trying to figure out why all his girls were so unhappy. Then I said, "What is going on here? How can it be that Christmas Eve in our home is feeling like it did when I was a kid and all the adults were arguing?" At that moment, my husband and I looked at each other, and my mouth dropped when he said: "It's because you invited them all here." Since that day, I am always careful that when I invite the spirits of my deceased relatives, I make sure they liked each other when they were living.

Every culture has its holiday traditions, customs, and food. Major holidays and minor holidays are all marked by a special meal or food. Because Italy is so diverse, these customs differ from region to region.

January

Capodanno (New Year's Day)

Originally, a *modenese* (from Modena) dish, *cotechino e lenticchie* is now enjoyed throughout Italy. It is eaten on New Year's Eve and is believed to bring prosperity for the new year. Lentils are disc shaped and thought to resemble coins. Pig (or pork) is an almost universal symbol of abundance. So strong is this belief that even people who do not care for the taste of cotechino will force themselves to eat one bite, not wanting to tempt fate and attract bad luck regarding their finances. The cotechino is a pork sausage made with pig's feet and skin and is robustly spiced. It is boiled or steamed for three hours (from raw) or twenty minutes (precooked). It is then sliced and served on a bed of lenticchie (lentils) cooked in vegetable broth and accompanied by some boiled potatoes.

Rest assured that pork sausage of any variety is a valid substitute. I've only cooked cotechino twice. Once over ten years ago and this year. The only reason I cooked it this year was that I forgot why I had cooked it only once previously. I hate it. I don't mind the gelatinous texture. It's the flavor. It is strong and gamey and just . . . not my thing. I eat many foods that are an acquired taste. I can't imagine ever acquiring the taste for cotechino. I even tried refrying the cooked, sliced cotechino with some onions and a splash of champagne. No. It was beyond redemption. The last time I threw out food was probably the first time I cooked cotechino. Anyway, I pulled a kielbasa out of the fridge, cooked it, and served that over lentils. Everyone was happy. I must confess that my husband and I did have a couple bites of the cotechino before it went into the trash. You know, taking one for the team, so to speak. Just in case the prosperity gods were watching.

February

Candelora (Candlemas)

Traditionally in Roman Catholicism, February 2 is the feast day of "The Presentation of Baby Jesus" and "The Purification of Mary." According to Jewish custom, women were considered unclean for forty days after the birth of a boy, and thus, they had to go to the temple to purify themselves. February 2 is exactly forty days after December 25, the birth of Jesus. Traditionally, it is also called Candlemas, because on this day blessed candles are burned symbolizing Christ. White candles are blessed by the priest and then taken home.

Years ago, when my husband and I were newlyweds, I was on the phone with my zia on February 2. My zia said to me wistfully: "Back in the day, we would ask the priest to bless a bunch of white candles. Too bad that the priests of today dismiss many of our traditions as superstition. If I were closer, I would bring you crêpes, three *confetti* (candy-coated almonds typically packaged in tulle and attached to a bonbonniere), and a blessed candle. The old ones would say that bringing these items to a young married woman guaranteed a baby within the year. The candle must be burned all the way down and any remaining wax collected. The wax and the confetti are placed on a clean handkerchief belonging to the husband and placed under the matrimonial bed." My zia was more than three hundred miles away. I didn't have crêpes that day, but magic is 100 percent intention, because exactly nine months plus a day later, we became parents for the first time.

In the following recipes, the measurements are part metric and part Imperial because that is the way they were related to me. Growing up Italian in Montreal, we not only mixed our languages, but we also mixed our measuring units!

Crêpes

Ingredients

250 grams flour

500 milliliters milk

1 pinch of salt

50 grams butter

1 packet Italian vanilla sugar

4 extra large eggs

Optional: 1 tablespoon amaretto

1. Pour the flour into a bowl and add the milk and beat with a whisk.

2. Add the remaining ingredients except for the eggs.

3. After whisking the mixture, add the eggs after beating them a little in a separate bowl and whisk to blend.

4. Let the batter rest in the refrigerator for an hour; then grease a pan with a little oil.

5. Now, cook the crêpes as you would pancakes.

6. You can fill and roll up the cooked crêpes with jam, chocolate, custard, whipped cream, etc.

March

Zeppole di San Giuseppe *(Saint Joseph's Donuts)*

This very traditional and simple recipe comes from my relatives from Napoli. Zeppole are traditionally made on March 19, the feast day of Saint Joseph, but there is no reason why you can't enjoy them year-round.

Ingredients

1 envelope or 2 teaspoons fast-acting yeast

2 teaspoons sugar

²/₃ cup milk

1 cup flour

Zest of 1 lemon

Pinch of salt

Icing sugar for sprinkling

1. In a large glass, dissolve yeast and sugar in lukewarm milk.

2. Let stand in a warm place for fifteen minutes.

3. Into a large greased bowl, pour the leavening mixture and add the flour, lemon zest, and pinch of salt. Stir until blended into a sticky batter/dough.

4. Cover the bowl with plastic wrap and place in a warm place for forty-five minutes to one hour. The batter will almost quadruple in quantity and have a nice spongy texture.

5. Heat vegetable oil to 350 degrees. Once the oil is hot, drop tablespoons of the batter two to three at a time.

6. Fry the zeppole until they float to the top of the oil and are golden all around.

7. Place cooked zeppole on a rack or paper towel.

8. When you finish making all your zeppole, sprinkle them with icing sugar.

April

Agnello con casce e ova (*Lamb with Cheese and Egg*)

This traditional recipe comes from Abruzzo and is prepared at Easter.

Ingredients

3 tablespoons extra virgin olive oil

1 sprig fresh rosemary (if you don't have fresh, season your meat with 1 tablespoon dried rosemary needles or ½ teaspoon ground rosemary)

1 clove garlic

Meat of 1 leg of lamb, cut up in one-inch cubes

1 glass dry white wine

4 eggs

2½ ounces pecorino cheese, grated

Juice of ½ lemon

Salt and pepper to taste

1. Place the extra virgin olive oil, a clove of garlic cut in half, and the sprig of rosemary in a pan and saute until the garlic is a little golden.

2. Remove the garlic and the rosemary and set aside.

3. Add the lamb cubes and brown over high heat on all sides.

4. When the lamb is browned, return the garlic to the pan and add the rosemary and white wine. Cook on low heat with the lid on for about half an hour.

5. When the lamb is cooked and tender, remove the rosemary.

6. In a small bowl, beat the eggs, add the grated cheese and lemon juice, and pour this mixture over the cooked lamb. Stir well to distribute the sauce and cook the egg.

7. Add pepper to taste and be careful to taste before adding salt because pecorino is very salty. Serve piping hot!

November: Il mese dei morti (The Month of the Dead)

Ossa dei morti (Bones of the Dead Cookies)

This traditional hard almond cookie is customarily baked and eaten during the entire month of November. The recipe is from the Abruzzese side of my family.

For best results, follow this recipe exactly as it is written and weigh all your ingredients in grams on a kitchen scale. One year I made these cookies the shape of little bones and gave them to my mail carrier, without any explanation. She mistook them for dog treats. Her Irish Wolfhound loved them!

Ingredients

2 eggs

300 grams ground almonds (weigh whole almonds on a kitchen scale and then blitz them in a food processor)

300 grams flour

300 grams sugar

½ teaspoon baking powder

Zest of 1 lemon

1. Preheat oven to 350 degrees Fahrenheit.

2. Beat the eggs in a bowl.

3. In another bowl, blend the ground almonds, flour, sugar, and baking powder.

4. Gradually add the wet mixture to the dry mixture.

5. Knead well until the mixture is smooth and add the lemon zest.

6. Roll out the dough and cut it in the shape of bones.

7. Bake for twenty-five to thirty minutes or until just starting to become golden.

Serve with a nice hot cup of Italian coffee for dunking.

December: La vigilia di natale (Christmas Eve)

Traditionally, Italians eat fish on Christmas Eve. Recall the Italian American tradition of the Feast of the Seven Fishes I described earlier. I can't say for sure that we ate exactly seven varieties of fish on Christmas Eve, but we certainly ate fish. My favorite is spaghetti with clams the way my zia from Naples prepared it without tomato.

Spaghetti con le vongole (Spaghetti with Clams)

Ingredients

    2 pounds fresh clams

    Olive oil

    1 or 2 cloves garlic

    1 pound spaghetti imported from Italy

    1 bunch fresh Italian parsley

    Salt and pepper

1. Inspect all your clams. Make sure they are not open or broken. Use only the clams that are shut tight. Discard those that are broken or already open.

2. Rinse the clams under running water and use a vegetable brush to remove any sand or debris from the clamshells. Place your clams in a colander to drain.

3. Pour a little olive oil into a large pot.

4. Add a peeled garlic clove and, on medium heat, warm the oil until the garlic is golden.

5. Drain the clams well and place them into the pan.

6. Put the lid on the pot and turn the burner up to high. Wait five minutes and check the clams. Cook until they are all

open and then turn down the heat to medium and keep cooking five more minutes. You will see a beautiful clam broth in your pot.

7. Remove the clams and set them aside on a plate.

8. Put the lid back on the clam broth and turn off the heat.

9. Cook the spaghetti to a minute less than the recommended time on the package.

10. While pasta is cooking, finely chop the parsley.

11. Then into a large pan, pour a little oil and add a clove of garlic.

12. Warm up the oil until the garlic clove is soft.

13. Strain the clam broth through a fine sieve and add it to the oil. Simmer for about five minutes. Turn off the heat.

14. To the clam broth, add the chopped parsley, drained spaghetti, and a ladle or two of the spaghetti cooking water. Add the clams and gently toss to coat and warm it all up.

15. Add some whole fresh parsley and some black pepper.

Turn off the heat and enjoy your spaghetti with clams!

Chapter 4

Witchcraft
or Medicine?

I am a registered nurse by profession. I am also a holistic practitioner and Reiki Master. I consider myself a well-rounded health-care professional and a relentless skeptic. In my thirty years of nursing experience, I have had the good fortune to witness and experience what could be best described as miracles. After witnessing and experiencing firsthand countless alternative medicine remedies—without an ounce of scientific backing or logic—treat, heal, and even cure disease, it finally occurred to me that in many cases what cannot be explained by science was in fact magic.

My paternal grandmother, Nonna 'Raziè—short for Graziella, a diminutive of her full name Maria Grazia; I am her namesake—was a healer, midwife, and psychic in her little mountain village in Abruzzo. People from her town and all the surrounding villages would make the journey, often on foot, up a steep mountain road to seek her help and counsel. As a result, I grew up with stories of remedies that dated back to the Middle Ages. Many of these ancient remedies were considered barbaric (torturous or dangerous to people and involving animal sacrifice) by sensibilities in Nonna's day; just imagine today's. For example, one ancient remedy for fever involved binding a live frog to the forehead with a bandage until the fever subsided. If the frog died, it was replaced with another live frog until the patient got better. My nonna replaced the frog with a potato.

It has always been interesting to me how she took these ancient, often unsafe, and barbaric remedies and updated them. What really fascinates me is that her updated remedies worked. Even more interesting is how I have, when necessary, for safety and hygiene, adapted her already-adapted remedies, and they have worked. Perhaps the magic resides in the fact that she kept and now I keep in mind the original ancient remedy. Or maybe it is the magic inherent in the healer. Whatever it is, it works and I don't like to look too closely at anything that works for fear it will stop working.

In my family and community, witchcraft and medicine are two sides of the same coin. In matters of wellness and illness, there are two points of view. There are members of my family and community who, upon experiencing ill health, will assume it is witchcraft until witchcraft is ruled out by a trusted spiritual healer. If witchcraft is ruled out or, in some cases, dealt with and symptoms persist, only then will they seek medical attention.

Conversely, there are people in the opposite camp, who, upon onset of ill health, will run to seek medical intervention. If the treatment prescribed is not effective, they may conclude that it is not a physical illness and therefore must be witchcraft. The idea is the doctor just ruled out a physical ailment, and therefore, their affliction must be the result of witchcraft.

The matriarchs and patriarchs of my family and community often boasted that the remedies they were sharing with me were ancient. The thing I found most interesting is that they all had so much in common no matter what region of Italy they hailed from. As I delved more deeply into the art of witchcraft and folk medicine, I learned that the commonalities were among not just other Italians, but other countries and cultures as well. My Ukrainian, Cuban, and Haitian neighbors practiced or at least knew of similar remedies in their own cultures. This is where my fascination with pathology (the study of illness) and pharmacology (the study of medication's effect on pathology and the body) was born.

Currently, we have a plethora of alternative medicine modalities at our disposal and many people who testify to their effectiveness, even though there seems to be no scientific reason as to why they worked. I decided a long time ago not to fret about the how and why and to just celebrate the results. If a natural or alternative remedy is safe, I'm open to it. My caveats are simple: the "medicine" must be safe and no living creatures harmed. I will clarify my second caveat during this chapter.

I titled this chapter "Witchcraft or Medicine?" because many of the treatments I will share with you either have no basis in science as we know it, or they are, in fact, magic spells. I have always thought that the folk medicine remedies that work without a clear indication of how, work by magic. They continued to be handed down for centuries because people felt they worked. You may also have a few folk remedies up your sleeve that would never be prescribed by your family doctor, but that your entire family practices and relies on because they are effective.

Approaches or Actions Taken for Every Condition

The following are really well-known approaches to remedy whatever ails you:

» Environmental interventions: Opening windows to *cambiare l'aria*; fumigating; cleaning; blessing; experiencing nature, fountains, rivers, lakes, oceans, sun, moon, wind; taking a journey to a place of power and then taking a different route home.

» Mental interventions: Changing one's focus or the subject of a conversation, venting, singing.

» Physical interventions: Engaging in physical exercise, bathing, anointing with oil, laying on of hands, receiving massage, seeking warmth, taking medicines (topical and ingested), eating the right foods.

» Spiritual interventions: Going to confession or visiting with clergy; seeking spiritual counseling from someone who the afflicted feels has power but who is not clergy; lighting candles and praying (some feel that attending Mass helps); making a pilgrimage to places of power (for example, those in Montreal may soak in the energy of Saint Joseph's Oratory; places of power can also be natural places of power—for example, the ocean).

Medicines

The following herbs and animal products described are local or indigenous to my paternal grandmother's region. As stated earlier, her medicines were adapted from medicines handed down and dating back as far as the 1100s. My nonna did not have any kind of formal medical training. She modified ancient remedies based on her own experimentation, which included trial and error. She developed medicines like her mother before her, who modified the medicine handed down to her from her mother, and so on. Medicines and remedies are modified mainly by necessity. The healer has to use what is available to her. The most interesting thing about these remedies is how the line between witchcraft and medicine is blurred because of the use of incantations.

I have further modified and added to my nonna's remedies based on my education and experience. I will never use a remedy that is unsafe or even questionable. This is the beauty of an oral tradition. Each generation modifies and adds to it.

Supplies and Tools of the Ancient Healer

I thought it would be fun to share with you some of the historical supplies and tools used by *gli antichi* (the ancient ones) because it's neat to get inside their heads as to why they used what they used.

Air: mountain, sea

Animals: pill bugs, black hens, black wolves, frogs, scorpions

Herbs: hypericum, bistort (snakeweed), verbena, oak bark, rue, rosemary, basil, oregano, spikenard, onion, garlic

Light: sun, moon, fire

Objects: spindle (especially the hub of the spindle), comb, sheep's wool, flour bin lid (looked like a shield)

Oil/Fat: lamp oil, fat from a black wolf, fat from a black hen

Salt

Water: well, spring, sulfur, lake, river, holy

My nonna lived in the mountains of Abruzzo in central Italy. Historically, this region was a pastoral society with sheep being the main livestock. It was very common to lose sheep, shepherd dogs, and the occasional hunting dog to wolves; therefore, wolves that dared to cross the path of any shepherd were hunted down and killed. So as not to waste anything, the wolf meat was fed to the dogs, the pelt made into clothing, and the fat rendered for medicine. My dad explained it this way: "Wolves hunted and ate our sheep. Wolves killed (and sometimes ate) our dogs. Therefore, the fat on their bones belonged to us. We were just taking back what was ours."

Fast-forward to a generation or two ago, and we see the substitutions and evolution:

Air: mountain, sea

Animals (no live animals): eggs, feathers, pure wool, gelatin, lard, animal bones and carcasses

Herbs: hypericum, bistort (snakeweed), verbena, oak bark, rue, rosemary, basil, oregano, spikenard, black pepper, hot chili pepper, cinnamon, ginger, cloves, nutmeg, onion, garlic, chicory, dandelions, mallow, rose, lilies, wildflowers, and the list goes on (we use what is available to us)

Light: sun, moon, fire

Objects: water, stones, earth, sand, herbs, from places of power

Oil: lamp oil (paraffin), olive oil, candle wax, vegetable shortening (lard does the same thing)

Salt

Water: well, spring, sulfur, lake, river, holy

Assessment and Diagnosis

Head

The belief is that when the head is affected, malocchio is most likely the cause.

Symptoms include headaches, migraines, confusion, anxiety, a feeling of impending doom, a feeling of being mentally and emotionally unsettled, lethargy, visual disturbances, or eye problems.

Therefore, first rule out malocchio or psychic attack. To check for malocchio, you use the water and oil method (found under "How to Diagnose Malocchio Using Water and Oil" in chapter II). If malocchio is present, remove it. Wait fifteen minutes and reassess the patient. I never cease to be amazed by the surprising number of symptoms/ailments that can be resolved by a simple malocchio removal.

If these symptoms are not alleviated by removing malocchio, they indicate a physical ailment. The following are some of the most common remedies and incantations for such ailments. I include the original incantations in the regional Italian dialect and offer a translation in English. I personally feel that incantations are most powerful in their original language. However, I have also witnessed them working perfectly fine when recited incorrectly or when translated to another language. Intent is key.

Headache

Headaches are believed to almost always be a symptom of malocchio.

People prone to headaches should wear a red headband or ribbon, *fettucce di Sande Silvestre* (Saint Silvester's ribbon), wrapped around the head and across the forehead and temples. This incantation is repeated three times, and with each repetition, the healer draws an *X* with their index finger on the afflicted person's forehead:

Sande Dunate, lu dolore de lu cape,

Sande Silvestre, lu dolore de la teste,

'N nome de Ddi, e de Sande Marije,

'N nome de Ddi, e tutte li sande,

Lu dolore se ne pozza ji.

Saint Donato, the head ache,

Saint Silvester, the head pain,

In the name of God and Saint Mary,

In the name of God and all the saints,

May the pain go away.

Head Cold, Sore Throat, or Bronchitis

For these ailments, rinse the mouth and gargle with warm water with salt added. Eat raw garlic and hot chili peppers to *ammazza' I migri'* (kill the germs). Apply *impacchi caldi* (cloth dipped in warm oil) to the neck and chest.

Tonsillitis or Swollen Glands

As for sore throats, first gargle with salt water to *disinfettare* (disinfect). Follow by gargling with barley water (water that has been used to cook barley) to soothe. Then wrap the neck with a wool cowl or scarf. Finally, recite the following prayer or incantation to San Biagio (Saint Blaise):

Sante Biage de nove fratelle

Da nove, è remaste otte

Da ott', è remaste sette

Da sett', è remaste sei

Da sei, è remaste cinghe

Da cinghe, è remaste quattre

Da quattre, è remaste tre

Da tre, è remaste ddu

Da ddu, è remaste une

Sante Biage squajje sti ghiannele.

Saint Blaise (one) of nine brothers

From nine, eight remained

From eight, seven remained

From seven, six remained

From six, five remained

From five, four remained

From four, three remained

From three, two remained

From two, one remained

Saint Blaise, melt these glands.

Muscle Aches

For muscle aches, take a hot bath with a fistful of salt added, followed by massage with warm oil. Dress warmly and avoid drafts.

Joint Pain (Arthritis)

For this ailment, keep parts of the body prone to arthritis warm. Massage the area with warm oil and cover with clothing made of wool—even in the summer.

Infection

If an area on the skin is infected or is at risk of becoming infected, rinse the area with salted water and apply an ointment made of one part raw garlic paste and two parts olive oil.

X and +

How many times have you pointed at someone's or your own body when describing another (third) person's ailment or tumor? Stop doing that right now and don't ever do it again. Our hands have intention and power in them. I was taught to never, ever, touch myself or someone else when describing illness. If I can do it even though my occupation requires I discuss patients' ailments all the time, you can do it.

Recently, I was in a meeting with a medical doctor friend of mine who was describing one of his patients while the entire time pointing at his own body in the places that his patient had illness. It took a lot of willpower for me to stay present in our conversation, while mentally and secretly drawing X's on each of his body parts that he pointed at. Not to mention the self-control I had to harness not to blurt out: "STOP POINTING AT YOUR BODY!"

Drawing an X banishes the *malvaggio* (or evil) that causes or feeds illness.

Drawing a + (plus) sign blesses and places healing energies on whatever you drew the + upon.

When you are healing someone, it is customary to trace an *X* three times on the injured site using the index finger of your dominant hand and then to trace three + signs with the index finger of your dominant hand to bless it with healing. In situations where you need to be more discreet, visualizing tracing the *X*'s and +'s in your mind is also effective.

N'è nient (Abruzzese dialect)

Non è niente (Italian)
[Non-EH-nyentay] (It is nothing.)

These three magic words are the most powerful incantation handed down to me. So powerful is this healing incantation that I only recall a handful of times it didn't work. Can you imagine an incantation that is so powerful that it rarely ever does not work?

I invoke *N'è nient* for everything—from paper cuts to quadruple bypass surgeries.

I'm a nurse, so I have had countless opportunities to put "It is nothing" to the test. At one time, I was a community wound-care nurse. I looked after chronic wounds, providing what in medical terms we call palliative wound care to wounds that doctors did not expect to heal. Yet, time and time again, I would witness complete healing. I approached every new wound with the same detached, almost dismissive, attitude. I would look upon the wound and say to myself, "It is nothing." And literally like magic—much to my amazement, because to be honest this never gets old—wounds that for years would not heal, did.

In the most dire and stressful circumstances, "It is nothing" seems to halt the negative momentum and suck it right out of the room.

Depending on the individual, "It is nothing" can be very reassuring coming from someone whose authority in the matter at hand we respect. For instance, my zia was not a doctor or a nurse, but when she said, "N'è nient," I believed her and it was always nothing.

In the case of extreme situations where the illness is terminal or fatal, n'è nient helps to bring us back to focus on the present moment. When experiencing the terminal illness of those close to me, human or canine, every day was a series of "It is nothing." This allowed space for wellness even in a terminal illness. It allowed space for meeting immediate needs of comfort, such as preparing a special meal or sharing a special moment. In extreme cases, the reassuring phrase n'è nient provides emotional and spiritual support to help us carry on with the business of living.

Chapter 5

Nature

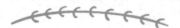

*Z*i' Francesco's house was a five-minute walk from my house. We lived in the city, but you couldn't tell once you entered his backyard. Tall hedges grew around his yard, blocking out the busy city street and serving as soundproofing against the city buses that stopped just in front of his house every five to ten minutes. In the summer, his garden grew every vegetable, herb, and fruit imaginable. He had a duck pond always occupied by wild ducks. In his trees, I saw birds I'd never seen. We only had sparrows in our nearby backyard.

I visited my uncle and aunt in the summer from the time I was six until the summer I turned twelve. Zi' Francesco's wife, Zia Maddalena, always insisted I stay for lunch. Then she would collect tomatoes, cucumbers, green onions, and basil from the garden and head inside. In no time, she was back with a huge bowl of tomato cucumber salad and a giant slab of her white pizza she had baked that same morning. White pizza is pizza dough topped with olive oil, salt, and pepper. There was nothing like Zia Maddalena's white pizza dunked in the juice that formed at the bottom of the salad bowl. If there was any salad left over, it was buried in the ground at the foot of the largest tree. The pizza crumbs were meticulously collected from the table and tossed on the grass. The first time I saw them do this, I asked: "Why do you bury the leftover salad and toss the bread crumbs on the grass?"

"The salad won't keep, and it is a shame to throw it in the garbage. We bury it at the base of the first tree we planted to give thanks for all we have and as an offering to ensure we will continue to always have what we need."

I loved visiting them and learning about gardening and communing with nature. Aside from the birds, squirrels, and insects that lived there, their entire garden felt like a benevolent spirit. They lived on a busy city street, yet the moment I entered their garden, I entered a peaceful wonderland. Every time I went through their gate to go home, the sight of the busy street and the noise of a bus stopping right out front were always jarring.

Zi' Francesco and Zia Maddalena had a relationship with everything in their garden. The trees and plants, the wild animals that visited, the insects, the soil, the rocks, the water, and the sun. They could forecast the weather better and more accurately than the TV weatherman! They loved nature and nature loved them back. Zia Maddalena confided to me that whenever she was worried about something, she would go out to her garden and unburden herself with the plants and animals. Then she would wait. She always received an answer. On one occasion, she was worried about her son. He was having trouble finding work, and she was worried her grandchildren were hungry. A few days after she had prayed in her garden, a family of squirrels appeared. There was a father, mother, and two young squirrels—just like her son's family. She quickly ran into her house and got a handful of nuts and placed it at the base of the tree where the squirrels were hanging out. The following Saturday she told me that her son was offered an even better job than the one that had laid him off.

The most fascinating inhabitant of their garden was a huge black crow. It was bigger than a house cat and perched on Zi' Francesco's shoulder when he was there. I was afraid of it, because at my house, black birds were a bad omen. They meant someone in the family was going to die. When the crow, named Zi' Nicola, came near me, I would shriek and run into the house to hide. Zia Maddalena would laugh and give me a hug and say, "Zi' Nicola probably wants your little gold hoop earring. Crows love shiny objects." Well, that just made me terrified that he was going to rip them out of my ears!

I went home one summer day after visiting Zi' Francesco and Zia Maddalena, and my aunt whom I lived with said: "Did you lose an earring?" I quickly felt my earlobes and discovered I was missing the left one. I removed the right one and put it away. That October, I was visiting Zia Maddalena on a Sunday afternoon. When I entered the garden, she was there, and so was Zi' Nicola. Zi' Nicola cawed and flew away. Minutes later he returned and landed on the picnic table. He had something in his beak. He placed it on the table and cawed. Zia Maddalena walked over and picked up the object. Then she walked to me and said, "Zi' Nicola found your earring!" I was so happy that I forgot my fear and reached over and stroked Zi' Nicola. Then we made eye contact, and it was like meeting a new friend. After that day, he would sometimes visit me in my backyard, much to my other zia's concern that someone was going to die because of his visit.

Zi' Francesco taught me that if I am afraid of or dislike anything in nature, it means I need to work on my relationship with that thing.

To this day, I continue to have a relationship with crows and ravens. Although I have since moved across the country, wherever I go, there they are. Here is a more recent example.

Every morning, crows would congregate in the sunlight on the back porch of my previous home. One day I happened to say to one very dapper-looking crow through my open kitchen window, "My, my, aren't you a handsome fella?" After that day, every time I saw the crows around my home, one or two would strut with their wings open, until I would say how handsome they were. Once I did, they would caw and fly away.

When I went to my car after work, a few miles away from my home, there would often be a crow on the hood of my car. I would walk up to my car, say, "Hey, buddy." I'd start my car and wait a moment for the crow to fly away. Then I noticed more and more crows near my parked car after work. I wondered to myself if they weren't the crows that lived in the trees behind my home, miles away from there. They seemed to know me.

Parking at my job was a challenge every morning. The parking lot was small and it filled up fast. Students and instructors arrived early for fear they would have to park in the street and plug a parking meter all day. However, whether I arrived early, on time, or a little later, the spot where I liked to park was almost always free. Even when the lot was full.

One morning, I pulled into the parking lot just as another car was leaving. The other driver said to me: "There isn't any parking, except for that one spot that always has about a dozen crows on it. I honked my horn and tried to shoo them away. They won't move, and I'm not running over a bunch of black birds." I drove to the spot to check it out for myself. The spot in question was my favorite spot, and it was, in fact, covered in crows. Just as I was about to drive away, I heard a caw. I looked, and they all walked out of the parking spot as an organized group. I said, "Thanks, guys," and parked my car. As I walked into work, a man smoking a cigarette on the street corner said to me: "I see them every morning. They are all in the parking spot until seconds before you show up. I'm starting to think they guard that spot just for you. You must be some kind of a witch or something."

A year later, I moved away from that house and changed jobs. It made me sad to leave my crow friends. When I arrived at my new home, I got out of my car and looked around. Suddenly, I heard a croaking sound. I looked up in the direction of the croaking, and there was a pair of very large ravens snuggling on the street lamp right beside my new home. This reassured me that I had made the right move.

I grew up in the city, yet I cannot remember a time when my elders were not talking about nature. There were two distinct and confounding messages:

» The God of the Roman Catholic religion controlled nature. He was responsible for creating everything from amoebae to natural disasters.

» Mother Nature was her own entity, and the "old ones" described her as God's wife. God was our physically absent omnipotent father in heaven, and Mother Nature was our ever-present mother who interacted with us through our environment. We were their children. (A child's first relationship is with their mother.)

The adept Italian witchcraft practitioner carries out their work through nature and with nature. It all begins with loving nature. We bring nature into our homes by opening windows and letting the sunshine in; using fireplaces and wood ovens; decorating with plants, fountains, wood, and stone; and having pets. The four elements are present throughout our homes, and we work with them daily. A practitioner's power is commensurate to the love they have for, and the devotion they have to, nature. The stronger the relationship, the stronger the practitioner's magic.

One thing you can do right now to develop a relationship with nature is to mindfully take care of plants and animals. Mindfully caring for your plants and animals is serving nature. Serving nature is a spiritual practice. It is through the spiritual practice of serving nature that I experience the interconnectedness of the universe that surrounds me. It is through my relationship with nature that I experience the creative force, the spark that connects the universe. It is my relationship with nature that helps me understand my own personal power.

How to Develop a Relationship with Nature

Plants

I used to think of myself as lacking a green thumb because my plants always died. I have lost count of how many plants and cacti I have killed. I believed that there were two kinds of people:

» People with a magical ability to grow anything

» Other people—like me—who, even after following instructions to the letter, had plants die

I would observe my dad tend to his plants, and he made it look so easy. For the life of me, I could not figure out what I was doing wrong. One day, after tossing out yet another dead plant, I expressed my frustration about how I was following the instructions that came with the plant or outlined in a reference book on plants and still my plants died. My dad looked at me from the tomato plant he was tying up to a pole and laughed. Then he said: "That is exactly what you are doing wrong. You can't learn how to take care of your plants from a book. You must develop a relationship with them. You serve them and they yield fruit. To develop this relationship, you must pay attention and give it what it needs. You do this by treating it like what it is, a living being, just like you."

There is something you can do right now to begin developing your relationship with nature. If you don't already have a plant, go out and get one. Once you have your plant, place it where you can see it all the time.

Name (or, as my dad would say, "baptize") your plant. Look at it and give it a name. For example, I have a plant named Boris. No one needs to know you named your plant, if you don't want them to. From this moment on, you will refer to your plant by its name, and when you speak to your plant, you will call it by its name.

The next step is to throw out all textbook plant-care instructions. This was a tough one for me because I get so hung up on following instructions. In this case, instructions are rigid and get in the way of your learning how to relate to and care for your plant. The only thing you need to keep in mind is what your plant needs to live and make sure it gets it. It needs water, food, sunlight, and love to thrive.

Next, ask your plant, "What can I do for you right now?" Then act on the message you receive. Inspect your plant. Do you think it could use some water? Do you think it would like more direct sunlight? If at first you don't receive a mental or thought message, don't give up. Communication, whether it be with plants or people, takes work. But I'm willing to bet that your plant will reply.

Animals

Another way we relate to nature is through our relationship with both domestic and wild animals. The caveat is that this relationship cannot be solely on our terms. It must be with the utmost respect for the animal's true nature. We respect the true nature of an animal by not anthropomorphizing it. We do this by learning to understand animals' instincts and not applying human motivations to their actions.

I come from a long line of dog people. Dogs were my ancestors' steadfast companions for herding sheep and hunting wild game. Therefore, their dogs were specific in breed: hunting and herding breeds. Their dogs had jobs, and they cared for their dogs out of a sense of stewardship, responsibility, and love. They took care of their dogs with respect for their nature and with a sense of obligation because they relied on their dogs' loyalty and skill for their and their livestock's survival.

We nurture our relationship with nature by being mindful about our relationship with our pets and wild animals.

Care for your pets with their true nature in mind:

» Walk your dog daily and consistently because their true nature needs both the physical exercise and mental stimulation.

» When your outdoor cat shows up bearing gifts of dead mice or birds, recognize and acknowledge your cat's true nature.

» When one of your pair of guinea pigs passes away, feel empathy toward the surviving, grieving guinea pig. Their true nature is companionship. Be ready to step in and offer support and companionship.

The moment an animal's true nature or spirit is aware that you see it, every member of its species sees yours and a bond is formed. This is evidenced by people who have an affinity for communicating with animals.

Nurture your relationship with wild animals by noticing them. Witness their spirit and feel your heart well up with awe and joy when you see them. Observe them in their environment. Learn about them, and only if it is safe to do so, attempt to communicate with them. Witness their true nature and their true nature will see you. Once their spirit witnesses yours, you will find that suddenly you see them more frequently. With practice, you will be able to read the messages these animals send you. Sure, you can read about portents and omens in a book, but the book will never be as accurate or meaningful as the signs you interpret on your own.

Make offerings. Don't throw out stale bread or bread crumbs from the supper table. Toss them out for the birds. Don't throw out food or water. Bury the food and pour the water onto the soil.

The Natural World

Nature surrounds us, and she expresses herself in seasons, months, lunar phases, and weather. When I was a child, I would hear the adults speak of months as though they were people. I have found that I have favorite months. These are months I look forward to like an old friend visiting.

Keep a journal, and at the start of every journal entry, record the phase of the moon. After a couple of lunar cycles, look back at your journal entries and look for patterns in your mood and the moon. Go out at night and look at the moon. To truly connect to its magic, view the moon through the eyes of your ancestors who lived long before man landed on the moon. On a night when the moon is full, go outside and bathe in its milky glow.

Le forze della natura
(The Forces of Nature, a.k.a. The Elements)

Air: The air we breathe sustains us; without it, we die. Mountain and sea air are the first medicines. Whenever I felt restless or stressed, my zia always said: "Esci fuori and prende l'aria fresca che te cambije la mend'" ("Go out and get some fresh air; it will change your mind/mood").

Earth: My zii always said that working the soil and gardening lightened the heart and spirit better than attending Mass. They said they didn't need church in the summer because communing with nature was better than religion. Some described how they would "feel a lightness in their bodies," or lose awareness of themselves and become one with nature.

Fire: Don't be careless with fire. Respect fire. Don't neglect the hearth fire. Feed it wood if you need it to burn. Respectfully smother it with ash if you need to extinguish it.

Water: Don't waste water. Don't pollute water. Cherish water, for water is life. Water washes away all that is stagnant and unclean. Water heals.

Don't complain about the weather. Whatever is going on with the weather, be grateful. If it is raining and you dislike rainy days, think of all the benefits of rain.

We all have favorite months. Don't spend your nonfavorite months looking forward to your next favorite month. February is my first favorite month of the year. It contains special anniversaries and therefore feels special from day one to twenty-eight (and sometimes twenty-nine). I catch myself in January thinking about February. I work on my relationship with January by being mindful of how January feels. This mindfulness is another way of saying: live in the present and make every moment count.

Don't complain about the season. Don't spend a quarter of your life (in places with four seasons) hating or complaining about a season. Find the beauty in that season, acknowledge it, and participate in seasonal activities.

If you dislike a weather condition, month of the year, or season, that means you need to heal your relationship with it. When you heal your relationship with it, you heal a part of yourself.

Chapter 6

Superstitions and Proverbs

"Non è vero . . . ma ci credo."

"It's not real, but I believe in it."

As you know by now, my family and community are made up of aunts, uncles, cousins, *commare* (godmothers), and *compare* (godfathers) from different regions of Italy. Although there is a common theme, each region has its own flavor or take on these common customs and traditions.

When I was five, I went to live with my zia and zio. My zia, my father's sister, was from Abruzzo. My zio was from Naples. My zio's family opened for me a whole new world of relatives, language, food, customs, rituals, and magic.

One of my earliest memories from that time is of a trip to the hairdresser. Two aunts, a half-dozen girl cousins, and I all took a city bus to the hair salon. I had only been to a hairdresser once before with my mom during a trip to Yugoslavia.

This salon was nothing like the tiny shop my mom took me to. It was busy and loud. The sound of water running and hair dryers filled the entire room. Italian pop songs played on the radio, and everyone was gesticulating, speaking loudly and all at once in a dialect that was still very foreign to me. I was fluent in Italian, but my mom, who hailed from northern Italy, taught me formal Italian. I clutched my aunt's hand as I took it all in. My aunt looked down at me and, after looking me up and down, said in Italian: "You're wearing gold and coral earrings. Good, because this place is full of *vipere* (vipers)." Without missing a beat, I asked: "What is a viper?"

At that exact moment, a woman in a paisley pantsuit who looked a lot like Maria on *Sesame Street* stroked my hair and said: "Hello, my name is Angela; what is yours? Mamma mia, what beautiful thick hair you have! Would you like a lollipop?" My aunt went from having her attention on a friendly conversation with another aunt to her full attention on me and began yelling at Angela: "No, she does not want a lollipop" (I really did) "and what did I hear you say to this poor innocent child?" Angela said, "What are you talking about?" My aunt replied, "You know what you did. Now make it right." Angela, dismissing my aunt with a wave of her hand as she walked to the back of the salon, said, "It's fine; she didn't say thank you." When I heard Angela say that I didn't say thank you for the compliment, I became upset and said to my aunt, "It's not true! I did say thank you."

As soon as I said that, my aunt began yelling at me to quickly spit on the floor. I didn't want to because I was taught not to spit at all, because it is rude. "Spit on the floor, Mary-Grace!" "No! I don't want to get into trouble." "Spit on the floor!" I began to cry. By now it seemed everyone in the salon had stopped talking and all eyes were on me. My aunt knelt down in front of me and said, "Everything will be okay. Please spit on the floor, Mary-Grace." I finally spat on the floor, and everyone went back to what they were doing.

My aunt turned to me and answered my earlier question. "Vipers are people who put the eye on other people. That is why you had to spit on the floor." With that, it was now my turn to get my hair cut. I was told to raise my feet off the ground as my aunt swept under my chair, before the hairdresser began cutting my hair. My aunt stood near me the entire duration of the haircut. When I was done, my aunt meticulously collected all my hair and placed it in a little plastic sandwich bag with my name on it. She then tucked the little bag in her purse. She did the same thing for each of my cousins. One cousin, who also had a manicure done, collected all her nail trimmings and placed them in a little bag and tucked it in her bra.

It has been over forty years, yet this memory is so vivid that it feels like yesterday.

Let me walk you through this event in terms of the superstitions and *scaramanzia* in play. (*Scaramanzia* [scah-rah-mahn-zee-ah] is a word, formula, gesture, or action used to ward off the evil eye and bad luck.)

Compliments: If paying someone a compliment, you must always follow it with a blessing such as "s'a benedica" (" be blessed or God bless"). Otherwise, your compliment can inadvertently cast bad luck on the recipient. If you receive a compliment and the person did not follow it up with a blessing or the person complimenting you is a rival, do not thank that person, but even if you don't thank them, immediately spit on the ground to prevent being affected by their glance. We do not thank them because their compliments can be code for a malediction. We spit as a gesture of rejecting their poison or curse. It is also customary to spit on the ground three times for good luck whenever you feel you need it.

Earrings: It was customary for newborn baby girls to have their ears pierced and wear gold earrings to protect against both blindness and malocchio (the evil eye). Red coral is present in a lot of traditional jewelry because it is believed to protect the wearer against enchantment. This is why my aunt checked that I was wearing earrings.

Hair and Nails: Never let your trimmed hair and nails out of your sight. Make sure to collect everything and take it home and burn it. Otherwise, they can be used to cast strong controlling spells and curses on you. This also goes for your hair caught on your comb. It all has to be burned and the ashes disposed of in the trash.

Sweeping: Never intentionally or inadvertently sweep a broom over an unmarried girl's feet, no matter what age, because doing so will condemn her to a life of spinsterhood. The same with boys, or alternatively, it's believed that they will have much difficulty winning a woman's heart.

Vipere: People (especially women but they can be men) who are unapologetically envious of others and thus meddle in other people's lives. They are also able to intentionally cast spells with a simple glance or a seemingly innocuous phrase.

Superstitions are believed to affect us even before conception and accompany us throughout our lives and into the afterlife. My personal experience has been that the two regions of Italy most preoccupied with magic are Campania (the province of Naples and surrounding area) and the mystical island of Sicily, with Naples possessing the greatest trove of magical lore. Next, let's look at some superstitions from both regions.

Marriage

Young single women should never wear a ring on their left ring finger, or else they won't get married.

Young single women should never try on another woman's wedding ring on their left ring finger. Doing so will cause the young single woman to never marry, and the married woman who let her try on her ring will be widowed within the year.

It is bad luck for the groom to see the bride in her wedding dress, except at the front door of the church on their wedding day.

The matrimonial bed must never be replaced, unless it is in such terrible condition that it can no longer be used. Replacing the bed without good reason could decrease the affection and love between the couple.

Never get married on a Tuesday. Historically, Tuesdays are considered cursed, and getting married on that day could jeopardize future happiness.

Conception

Conceiving a child during a waxing or full moon favors a female child. Waning moon, especially waning quarter crescent moon, conceptions favor males.

Pregnancy

Never announce a pregnancy before the expectant mother is showing or, at the very earliest, after completing the first trimester. It is bad luck and can cause a miscarriage.

Cravings must be satisfied; otherwise, the baby will be born with a birthmark in the shape of the craving. Another version of this is that an expectant mother should never touch her body when craving something, or else the baby will have a birthmark in the shape of the craving on the same spot on its body. I craved coffee like crazy when I was pregnant with my eldest. She has a birthmark on her leg that looks like . . . a coffee stain.

Expectant mothers must avoid looking at anything ugly or malformed for fear their child will be born ugly or malformed.

Pregnant moms should never cut their hair for fear it may cause miscarriage . . . unless they are pregnant during the month of March. It is safe to get their hair cut the first Friday in March.

If a pregnant mom's belly is rounded and she is carrying low, she's expecting a girl. If her belly is pointed and she is carrying high, she's expecting a boy.

Pregnant moms should never wear necklaces for fear the baby's cord will wrap around its neck.

Pregnant moms should never cross their legs, or their baby will be born breech.

Morning sickness only the first trimester = boy. Morning sickness that persists the entire pregnancy = girl.

Heartburn means the baby will have a lot of hair.

Some believe a pregnant woman should never enter a cemetery for fear a wandering soul will take the place of her baby's soul, resulting in the baby's soul being trapped in limbo. The wandering soul may wander off before the baby is born. In this case, the baby will be stillborn. If the wandering soul sticks around, the infant will die within the first year.

Children

Newborn babies are given an amulet for protection against magic/evil eye from their godmother. This amulet is traditionally a red ribbon or coral bead on an eighteen-karat gold safety pin pinned to the inside of their clothing, although other configurations also exist.

Once the umbilical cord falls off, it is placed under the father's supper plate to ensure the child will never be late for meals. When the meal is done, the father buries the umbilical cord in the ground on the family property to ensure the child will always honor their family of origin.

The godmother is the first person to trim the newborn's nails. She then places a coin in the newborn's palm as a blessing for wealth.

Newborns are given an egg as a gift so they may grow to be a person of substance and are given salt for intelligence.

It is bad luck to celebrate a baby's *onomastico* prior to their first birthday. *Onomastico* is the Italian word for "name day." It is similar to one's birthday in that it is the tradition of celebrating the day associated with a person's given name; for example, September 29 is the feast day of Saint Michael, and everyone named Michael or a version of Michael celebrates their onomastico (name day).

Never place an infant in front of a mirror. To do so will cause speech and language delay.

Some people believe that you should never photograph a sleeping baby. To do so will result in the baby dying in their sleep.

Never cut a baby's hair until the child is at least a year old. The first haircut must occur on the first Friday in March for luck.

Little girls' braids are a symbol of good luck and therefore should be cut only after they turn eight or ten. After the braids are cut, it is best to preserve them (braided) or donate them to a saint as an offering (ex-voto).

Never step over a child lying on the floor. Doing so will stunt their growth. If you accidentally step over a child, stop and step back.

When a child loses a baby tooth, throw it as far as you can, while reciting: "San Nicola, San Nicola, vi dugnu lu vecchiu e mi dati lu novu" ("Saint Nicholas, Saint Nicholas, I give you the old and you give me the new").

Personal Well-Being

Never place your purse or wallet on the floor, or you will never have any money.

When talking about illnesses, never touch your own or someone else's body, or the body you touch will develop the same illness.

If you hear sirens or see a hearse, touch gold to ward off misfortune.

Never imitate a person with a handicap, or misfortune will befall you.

If you receive a mirror as a gift, the person giving the mirror must be paid. A penny suffices. The purpose is to transfer ownership of the mirror in case it shatters. This is to prevent the recipient from using the gift to curse the giver with the mirror. Also, if the mirror should break accidentally, the recipient "owns" the bad luck.

Always avoid giving knives, scissors, or cutting tools because they symbolize cutting ties. If you give such a gift and you want to avoid the consequences, then the receiver needs to pay you a nominal fee, such as a small coin.

It is bad luck to allow a candle to burn itself out. Always extinguish the candle before it is done.

The number 13 is lucky. The only exception is to never set a table for thirteen people (as done at the Last Supper).

The number 17 is unlucky.

Never begin a new project or go on a trip on a Tuesday. It will not be successful.

It is bad luck to wear a new article of clothing for the first time on a Friday.

When your left hand is itchy, you will receive money. If your right hand is itchy, you will pay money. Alternatively, if your right hand is itchy, you will give a beating. If your left hand is itchy, you will receive a beating.

If you drop an object a few times in succession, an unexpected visitor will appear shortly.

When you are getting dressed in the morning, if you accidentally put your clothes on backward or inside out, it is good luck and you will receive good news.

Always make the sign of the cross when yawning to prevent evil spirits from entering your body through your mouth.

It is good luck to run into a priest on your path. It is bad luck to run into nuns on your path.

When a young man was called to military service in the Navy, his mother had to dip a mop inside a tub of water and place it on the ground, on the balcony or terrace, covered by a sieve, in the sun. The first remedy (dipping the mop) served to calm the waters and the second (covering the mop with a sieve) to mitigate the scorching rays of the sun, so that her son would not encounter any danger during his travels.

Never count your money before the game has ended, or else you will lose it all and more.

Never celebrate on a Friday unless it is the exact day of a holiday, birthday, or anniversary, since the old saying goes: "Cu ridi di venniri, chianci di duminica" ("He who laughs on Friday, cries on Sunday").

For good luck, climb a ladder on New Year's Day, beginning with your left foot.

A woman should never do the following when menstruating:

» Touch flower buds; they will not bloom.

» Knead bread dough; it will not have flavor.

» Touch preserved foods; they will spoil.

Food, Cooking, and Eating

When cooking with eggs, never discard eggshells halved. Always smash them with your palm first. Otherwise, you invite evil into your home.

Bread, both at the table and when stored, must always lie right side up and never turned upside down. This essential food is considered "the grace of God" and therefore must be respected and admired in all its beauty. If you accidentally place bread upside down, quickly pick it up and place it right.

When eating a meal, you must finish the piece of bread you began to eat or else lose one year of your life.

If a piece of bread falls to the ground, you must immediately pick it up and eat it, to avoid future hardships. If you do not want to eat it, you must kiss it before disposing of it.

Never place your cutlery crossed on your plate, or you will have many crosses to bear your entire life.

Discarding and wasting food will bring bad luck and famine.

The Home

It is bad luck to sweep your home after dark.

If you suspect someone is cursing you, place a broom, braided garlic, and a bunch of hot peperoncino peppers by your front door. Not only will the peppers prevent malocchio, but they will deflect the curse and afflict the sender.

Never change houses or buy a new broom in August.

Oil spilled on the table or floor is bad luck. Quickly cover it with a fistful of salt and wipe it up. Remember to toss a pinch of salt over your left shoulder with your left hand.

Accidentally spilling wine on the table is good luck. Wet your fingers with the spilled wine and dab it behind your ears.

Never place money on a table set for a meal. Doing so is inviting Judas (the apostle who betrayed Jesus) to the table.

Daisies by your front door attract abundance and prosperity.

When building a new home, you will have future prosperity and luck if you throw some coins in the foundation or in the concrete being poured for the floor. There is also the custom of offering builders a hearty lunch of pizza and pastries, after having completed the floor. You must cook and eat fried fish on your first day in your new home as a blessing for a peaceful future and recite this Sicilian saying: "Ncignari la casa cu li pisci fritti" ("Begin/start the house with fried fish").

Remove cobwebs with your left hand for good luck.

He who plants a little walnut tree will live a long life and die only when the circumference of the tree trunk matches the length of his belt.

Animals and Insects and Nature

Frogs, since ancient times, have always been considered the ideal vessel for the deluded souls of princesses or good mothers grieving over the loss of a son to retreat in. From this belief has arisen the belief that frogs must always be respected and never killed if you do not want to risk some sad event.

Lizards are considered blessed and therefore should not be killed.

Scorpions are considered evil. Sacrificing (killing) a scorpion releases you from any debt with dark forces.

To break free from evil spirits, all one has to do is kill a toad, which, unlike the frog, is considered an animal of the devil.

The bat, *taddarita* or *surci Vecchiu* in the Sicilan dialect, is considered an unclean and otherworldly animal. It is best to stay well away from bats and avoid hurting or killing them because doing so can result in misfortune.

To prevent misfortune, take care when killing a chicken to recite the following Sicilian spell: "La morti a tia e la saluti a cu ti mancia" ("Your death is health to those who eat you").

Killing a cat brings seven years of *disgrazia* (misfortune).

When a cat washes its face, it is going to rain.

If a red fly or a colorful butterfly enters your home, you will receive good news.

Another spell to calm the fury of the sea was to prepare a beautifully crafted *panino* (sandwich) decorated with rosemary and sesame and dedicate it to Saint Joseph. Kiss the panino and toss it at the waves, reciting the following prayer: "San Giusippuzzu cu la sciuruta parma, l'unni di lu mari prestu carma" ("Saint Joseph with the blossoming (open) palm (of his hand), the waves of the ocean (he) will soon calm").

Good and Bad News

The following are harbingers of good news:

» The sound of a musical instrument or singing in the middle of the night

» A rooster crowing

» Overhearing someone else's conversation about good news

The following are harbingers of bad news:

» A rival neighbor tossing dirty water into the street (there will be tears)

» A nearby donkey braying

> » Hearing someone wailing

> » Witnessing a bloody fight

> » The mournful hoot of an owl

> » The soft meowing of a cat

For good auspices and good luck, take palms braided with little olive branches that were blessed during Palm Sunday mass, and burn them with a little incense. Doing so on the morning of *Sabato Santo* (Easter Saturday) while reciting the following charm will serve as protection against malocchio.

Parma e uliva biniditta

nterra sì nata, 'ncelu sì scritta,

pi sta virtù ca Diu t'ha datu

lu malocchiu è trapassatu.

Blessed palm and olive

On Earth you were born, in Heaven you are written,

For this virtue that God has given you,

The malocchio has been overcome.

La Smorfia Napoletana (Neapolitan Dream Dictionary of Symbols Corresponding to Lottery Numbers)

Neapolitans have a dream dictionary called *La Smorfia* consisting of a list of words, each with a corresponding number for the sole purpose of playing the lottery. The word *smorfia* means grimace in Italian, but it is most likely a Neapolitan reference to Morpheus, the god of dreams. It is quite elaborate. Following is a sample of ninety things a person may dream about and their corresponding numbers. I learned this list playing *tombola* as a child. Tombola is a type of Italian bingo. Whenever a number was called out, so was the corresponding word or phrase. Quite often, the word would be called out instead of the number.

1   *L'Italia* – Italy

2   *'A Piccerella* – a little girl

3   *'A Jatta* – a cat

4   *'O Puorco* – a pig

5   *'A Mano* – a hand

6   *Quella che guarda verso terra* – she who is looking at the ground

7   *'O Vase* – a jar

8   *'A Madonna* – The Madonna

9   *'A Figliata* – offspring

10   *'E Fasule* – beans

11   *'E Suricille* – mice

12   *'O Surdate* – soldier

13   *Sant'Antonio* – Saint Anthony

14   *'O 'Mbriaco* – the drunk

15   *'O Guaglione* – the boy

16   *'O Culo* – ass (butt)

17   *'A Disgrazzia* – misfortune/bad luck

18   *'O 'Sanghe* – blood

19   *'A Resata* – laughter

20   *'A Festa* – the party

21   *'A Femmena annura* – the naked woman

22   *'O Pazzo* – the madman

23	*'O Scemo* – the fool
24	*'E Gguardie* – the guards
25	*Natal'* – Christmas
26	*Nanninella* – Anna
27	*'O Cantero* – the urinal
28	*'E Zzizze* – tits
29	*'O Pate d'e Ccriature* – the father of the children
30	*'E Ppalle d'o Tenente* – the lieutenant's balls (testicles)
31	*'O Padrone 'e Casa* – the landlord
32	*'O Capitone* – the eel
33	*L'Anne 'e Cristo* – years of Christ
34	*'A Capa* – the head
35	*L'Aucelluzz* – the bird
36	*'E Ccastagnelle* – the castanets
37	*'O Monaco* – the monk
38	*'E Mmazzate* – beatings (with a stick or a bat)
39	*'A Funa n'Ganna* – the noose
40	*'A Paposcia* – the hernia
41	*'O Curtiello* – the knife
42	*'O Cafè* – coffee
43	*Onna pereta fore 'o barcone* – woman on the balcony
44	*'E Ccancelle* – prison
45	*'O Vino bbono* – good wine
46	*'E Denare* – money
47	*'O Muorto* – the dead (person)

48	*'O Muorto che pparla* – the dead (person) that speaks
49	*'O Piezzo 'e carne* – piece of meat
50	*'O Ppane* – bread
51	*'O Ciardino* – the garden
52	*'A Mamma* – mother
53	*'O Viecchio* – the old man
54	*'O Cappiello* – the hat
55	*'A Museca* – music
56	*'A Caruta* – the fall (as in a person falling) or the fallen (person)
57	*'O Scartellato* – the hunchback
58	*'O Paccotto* – the packaging
59	*'E Pile* – hairs
60	*Se Lamenta* – complains
61	*'O Cacciatore* – the hunter
62	*'O Muorto acciso* – the dead man killed/murdered
63	*'A Sposa* – the bride
64	*'A Sciammeria* – the tailcoat
65	*'O Chianto* – crying
66	*'E ddoie Zetelle* – the two spinsters
67	*'O Totaro int'a Chitarra* – the squid in the guitar (two things that have nothing to do with one another)
68	*'A Zuppa cotta* – the cooked soup
69	*Sott'e 'Ncoppa* – upside down
70	*'O Palazzo* – the palace
71	*L'Ommo 'e Merda* – man of shit (a reprehensible man)

72   *A Maraviglia* — the amazement

73   *'O Spitale* — the hospital

74   *'A Rotta* — the cave

75   *Pullecenella* — Pulcinella is a character in Neapolitan puppetry that originated in the 17th century in the commedia dell'arte. He represents the voice of the people of Naples.

76   *'A Funtana* — the fountain

77   *'E Riavulille* — the little devils

78   *'A bella Figliola* — the prostitute

79   *'O Mariuolo* — the thief

80   *'A Vocca* — the mouth

81   *'E Sciure* — flowers

82   *'A Tavula 'mbandita* — table set for a meal

83   *'O Maletiempo* — bad weather

84   *'A Cchiesa* — the church

85   *'Ll Aneme 'o Priatorio* — the souls in purgatory

86   *'A Puteca* — the shop

87   *'E Perucchie* — lice

88   *'E Casecavalle* — the caciocavalli (cheese shaped like eights, plural)

89   *'A Vecchia* — the old woman

90   *'A Paura* — fear

Proverbs

A buon intenditore poche parole.
> Few words are needed when speaking to a good listener. (Those who understand do not require lengthy explanations.)

A pagare e morir c'è sempre tempo.
> No rush to pay or to die. (Unpleasant tasks are always left for last.)

Campa cavallo che l'erba cresce.
> Keep living horse, the grass growing. (A reminder to continue living your life while waiting for a favorable outcome.)

Carte scritte, cafone dorme. (Scripta manent, verba volant—Latin*)*
> When things are put in writing, the peasant sleeps. (Script remains, words fly.)

Chi disprezza compra.
> He who devalues something ends up purchasing it. (When a person, out of laziness, devalues with their words something they really appreciate. Sour grapes.)

Chi ha tempo non aspetti tempo.
> He who has time to do something should not postpone it until later. (The equivalent of "A stitch in time saves nine.")

Chi lascia la vecchia per la nuova sa quel che lascia ma non sa quel che trova.
> He who quits the old for the new knows what he has left, but not what he will find. (The equivalent of "The devil you know.")

Chi non risica non rosica.
> Nothing ventured, nothing gained. (If you don't risk anything, you don't gain anything.)

Chiodo schiaccia chiodo.
Nail crushes nail. (A new problem takes priority over an old problem.)

Chi si accontenta gode.
Those who are content with what they have, enjoy what they have. (An invitation to exercise moderation in your desires.)

Chi si scusa s'accusa.
He who excuses himself accuses himself. (When you apologize without being prompted by circumstances, it means that you feel guilty or are guilty.)

Chi va con lo zoppo impara a zoppicare.
Who goes with the lame learns how to limp. (We adopt other people's habits, especially bad ones.)

Dal mattino si vede il buon giorno.
From the morning we can tell a good day. (You can tell from the start whether or not an enterprise will be successful.)

Fatta la legge, trovato l'inganno.
As soon as the law is passed, we figure out a way to evade or break it. (There is always a loophole.)

Gallina che canta ha fatto l'uovo.
The hen that sings has laid an egg. (When someone appears happy for no reason, she is hiding something.)

Gobba a ponente luna crescente, gobba a levante luna calante.
Hump to the west, the moon is waxing, hump to the east, the moon is waning. (Nursery rhyme to remember lunar phases.)

Il diavolo fa le pentole ma non i coperchi.
The devil makes pots, but not lids. (No matter how devious the scheme [pot], you will always end up exposed [no lid].)

Il diavolo non è così brutto come si dipinge.

The devil is not as ugly as he is portrayed. (Often the things we fear are not so terrible.)

Il medico pietoso fa la piaga verminosa.

The doctor who takes pity allows the wound to fester. (Often situations escalate when you do not have the courage to take the appropriate action.)

Il mondo è bello perché vario.

The world is beautiful because it is varied. (An invitation to appreciate diversity.)

Il sangue non è acqua.

Blood is not water. (Blood is thicker than water.)

Il silenzio è d'oro e la parola è d'argento.

Silence is golden and words are silver. (Since gold is more valuable than silver, it is more valuable to be quiet than to speak.)

Il troppo stroppia.

Too much is too much. (Too much of a good thing can be harmful.)

Impara l'arte e mettila da parte.

Learn the trade and keep it stored. (Learn as many skills as you can.)

In compagnia prese moglie un frate.

In company, the brother (monk) took a wife. (Sometimes the company of certain people can make us do things that we would otherwise never do.)

La coda è la più lunga da scorticare.

The tail takes the longest to skin. (The final part of the work always feels like it takes the longest to do.)

La gatta frettolosa fece i gattini ciechi.

The hurried cat makes blind kittens. (Hurried work does not give good results.)

La lingua batte dove il dente duole.

The tongue always touches the sore tooth. (Thoughts and conversations often return on the topics that are most important to us.)

L'appetito vien mangiando.

Appetite comes while eating. (This proverb has two connotations. It may indicate that the more you have, the more you want. Or it may mean that there are things that we don't feel like doing that we begin to appreciate once we start to do them.)

La prima acqua è quella che bagna.

The first water is what wets. (The first impact of a negative experience is the worst. Then we get used to it—like when we jump into a swimming pool. The water feels cold at first; then we get used to it.)

Le bugie hanno le gambe corte.

Lies have short legs.

L'occasione fa l'uomo ladro.

Opportunity makes the thief.

Moglie e buoi dei paesi tuoi.

Wife and oxen of your country. (An exhortation to prefer things with which we are more familiar.)

Non c'è due senza tre.

There is no two without three. (This saying holds that if a thing has happened twice already—good or bad—it will happen a third time. That said, it is linked to the belief that the number three is a perfect number. "Everything happens in threes.")

Non c'è peggior sordo di chi non vuol sentire.
> There are none so deaf as those who do not want to hear. (There is no cure for the deafness of those who do not want to hear.)

Ogni lasciata è persa.
> Every left is lost. (Every opportunity that we have not taken is lost.)

Quando la neve si scioglie si scopre la mondezza.
> When the snow melts, the trash is revealed.

Quando la pera è matura casca da sé.
> When the pear is ripe, it falls on its own. (We need to be patient.)

Res non verba. (Latin)
> Deeds rather than words.

Scherza coi fanti e lascia stare i santi.
> Jest with knaves and neglect the saints. (Serious things are not to be taken lightly.)

Tempus omnia medetur.
> Time heals all wounds.

Tra moglie e marito non mettere il dito.
> Do not put your finger between husband and wife. (Do not interfere in disputes, especially if they involve people closely linked.)

Tutte le strade portano a Roma.
> All roads lead to Rome. (There is always a way, although winding, to reach our goal.)

Tutti i nodi vengono al pettine.
> All knots are caught by the comb. (You cannot hide your transgression. Curses are like chickens; they always come home to roost.)

Una mano lava l'altra e tutte e due lavano il viso.

One hand washes the other and both hands wash the face. (It is important to help one another.)

Una rondine non fa primavera

(The appearance of) one swallow does not make a summer (spring). (The swallow is a beautiful bird with a forked tail. Swallows are a harbinger of spring. One positive sign is not enough to make us believe that the situation will turn to the better.)

Uomo avvisato mezzo salvato.

Forewarned is forearmed. (An exhortation to heed the warnings that can help us avoid making mistakes.)

Chapter 7

Amulets and Talismans

As old as time itself, amulets are objects believed to banish bad luck and protect us from harm. Talismans are objects believed to bring good luck and attract desired outcomes. Italian amulets and talismans are almost all interchangeable. A luck charm's function is as amulet to ward off bad luck and talisman to attract good luck. This is why I choose to use the words *amulet* and *talisman* interchangeably unless the object is specifically one or the other. Amulets and talismans are objects often used in scaramanzia.

Here are some examples:

Amber: Fossilized resin used to make beads or gems worn by magicians for protection against evil spirits.

Braided garlic: This symbol of Saint Michael Archangel is a ward against evil spirits, *fatture* (curses), and malocchio. I describe braided garlic as a symbol of Saint Michael, but my ancestors described garlic as being literally an earthly manifestation of Saint Michael and not merely a symbol. Garlic *is* Saint Michael. Braided garlic can be placed outside the home by the front door with the broom.

Branches: Fallen branches (never taken) are a gift from tree spirits and protect the finder and their home from curses and misfortune.

Brass: Brass is used in love magic and spells to increase a woman's beauty and attractiveness, corresponding with the Roman goddess Venus.

Broom: When placed outside the home beside the front door, a broom wards against malocchio.

Coins (especially coins with a hole in them): Coins provide luck in games and lotteries.

Copper: Copper is used in love magic and spells to increase a woman's beauty and attractiveness; like brass, it corresponds with Venus.

Coral: Hard substance similar to rock. It is the skeleton of a type of sea creature. Coral is used in jewelry, and it is worn as a ward against the evil eye.

Corno: Amulet in the shape of a bull's horn or long chili pepper. This wards against malocchio; it also is a protection amulet for men to protect potency.

Desiccated sea horse: The sea horse wards against malocchio.

Dried herbs: Bunches of dried herbs can be hung on the wall of your home for various purposes. Rue protects against evil, basil is used for love and harmony, oregano is for prosperity, and rosemary is used to alleviate sadness/grief.

Earrings: Gold earrings are wards against blindness and malocchio.

Fabric: Fabric is used in the construction of *santucci* (charm bags) and various amulets and talismans. The color of the fabric must correspond with the purpose of the charm. For example, black is used for binding or banishing. Red is used for protection against enemies, witchcraft, and evil spirits. Green is used for love charms.

Gobbo: This figurine of a hunchback wearing a top hat where the bottom half of his body is a corno is typically found on a key chain. Rubbing a hunchback, either on a real person or on this good luck charm, is believed to protect against the evil eye. If you do see a person with a hump, please refrain from touching them without their permission. It's kind of weird. If you do know them, ask before touching. It's just good manners.

Gold: Gold wards against misfortune and malocchio. It symbolizes the power of the sun and masculine energy.

Hare/Rabbit's foot: This charm *must* be given to you by the person who killed the rabbit in order for it to be lucky.

Holy oil: This oil is used for healing and blessing.

Holy water: This water is used to exorcise and to bless.

Iron: Touching iron wards against misfortune. It is used in both defensive and offensive magic, corresponding with Mars.

Key: This wards against malocchio.

Knife: A knife is used in magic to cut ties, cut through lies, and get to the heart of the matter. This knife would not be used for any nonmagical purpose. This knife serves also as a powerful ward against curses. A father who felt he was nearing death would gift his knife to one of his children, usually the eldest son. In this case, the son or daughter does not pay the symbolic fee because the point of passing on the knife is to maintain the connection to ancestors through this object.

Lead: Lead is used in binding magic to "weigh it down," corresponding with Saturn.

Mano cornuto (The Horned Hand): This charm in the shape of a hand gesture with only the index and pinky finger pointing to look like horns of a bull protects against bad luck and malocchio. The hand gesture itself is protection.

La Manu Fica (The Fig Hand): Literally, this is a hand that does a gesture representing the vagina. The hand is closed in a fist with the thumb resting between the index and middle finger. The hand gesture itself was often used by the women in my family and community in the same way people give the middle finger as an insult. Also, a charm or pendant in the shape of this hand gesture is worn to protect against infertility in the same way the corno is worn by men to protect potency.

Nails (rusty or not): Nails may be used on their own or as part of an amulet. Often they are used in spells.

Needle: A needle is used for sewing and for protection against malocchio. It is also used in one of the many spells to remove malocchio.

Object once belonging to a deceased loved one: This item may be a piece of jewelry, a hat, a key chain, or a book, for example.

Peperoncini (long, red hot peppers) threaded or strung on a cord or kitchen twine like a beaded necklace: Strung peperoncini are both a good luck charm and a ward against curses and malocchio.

Saint medals: They can be as simple and inexpensive as the little saint medals sold at cathedral gift shops, or they may be custom made in eighteen-karat gold. Typically, one would wear (and *never* remove) a medal of their patron saint as protection against evil and malocchio.

Saint prayer cards: These laminated cards have a picture of a saint on one side and the novena prayer to that saint on the other. I have a "deck" of the saints I have a working relationship with that I use as a sort of oracle.

Saint relics: These are usually sealed, clear, soft plastic pouches with a picture of a saint and a tiny square of felt that touched the saint's remains. I have one of Padre Pio in my car. I have had a few really close calls driving over the years that I believe

I emerged from unscathed because of my relationship with Padre Pio and the relic that I keep in my car. (Padre Pio, born Francesco Forgione, was canonized in 2002 and now ranks among the most beloved saints.)

Salt: When I was a young girl and visited Naples, every store or business had a little bowl of salt on the counter beside the cash register. The storekeepers would sprinkle salt from that bowl on their countertop and floor a few times daily. The salt would be wiped off the counter onto the floor, and the salt on the floor would then be swept out of the store with the broom that was stored right by the entrance. This ritual was a ward against bad luck and malocchio. Salt is the most powerful weapon to dispel evil and is used in all types of amulets/talismans.

Sand: Sand contains the power of the ocean.

Sand dollars: These shells ward against malocchio.

Santucci [san-TOO-chee]: These little charm bags are made of felt or any other fabric similar in thickness about one inch by two inches. Inside, you place a little medal of the saint you are petitioning for a blessing or protection. The two sides are sewn together with the saint on the inside. Other small items are added depending on the type of amulet you are making, and then the two pieces of fabric are sewn together by hand.

Sea shells (to symbolize the Roman goddess of Love, Venus): Shells provide luck in love and are used in love amulets.

Silver: Silver wards against malocchio. It symbolizes moon energy and is a feminine energy.

Soil (from holy ground such as a church or a cemetery, or from places of power): Soil is used in santucci (charm bags) to enhance protection against curses.

Starfish skeletons: Starfish ward the home or business against malocchio.

Stones/rocks (especially stones with a hole in them): These are used for luck.

Thread: This thread is used for sewing santucci (saint charm bags/amulets). The color of the thread must be the same color as the fabric you are using.

Tools: Typically, the tools of one's trade are used. An example is a seamstress who uses primarily needles and scissors in her magic.

Water (from a stream, lake, river, ocean, or other living body of water): Water is used to cleanse and bless people and objects.

Wards placed indoors just above the entrance doors include crucifixes, horseshoes, corni (plural of corno), and red ribbons.

Here are some traditional objects and gestures used to protect against the malocchio:

» Wear a necklace with a small pouch containing some blessed salt, a nail, or a clove of garlic. Some people also like to add a tiny piece of palm or olive (branch) that was blessed on Palm Sunday.

» Always carry in your pocket one of the following: a nail, a red corno, a gobetto, or a horseshoe.

» Sew a small piece of red fabric or ribbon inside clothing you wear every day.

» Keep a string with a red hot peperoncino (like a Thai chili pepper) in your pocket.

» Wear a desiccated sea horse on a string around your neck.

» If you cross paths with a person you suspect means you harm, touch iron or else spit on the ground three times. If you are a man, discreetly touching your own genitals works.

» With your hand hidden in a pocket, make the hand gesture for manu fica. You can do the same by making the hand gesture of *mano cornuto* with both hands.

» Secretly make the sign of the cross on your palate with your tongue.

How to Make Amulets/Talismans

It wasn't that long ago that I was a young girl and we would attend *feste*—a block party to celebrate a saint in the area immediately surrounding our church. There were always vendors selling inexpensive saint medals and other souvenir type items. Often the same vendor selling saint tchotchkes also sold corno and gobbo figures on keychains. After making our purchases, we would head over to a table where our parish priest would bless everything—yes, even the items of superstition. We would all head home with our bellies full of fried dough and sausages, clutching our little bags full of blessed amulets.

Amulets obtained and not blessed by a priest had to be washed in soapy water with a pinch of salt in it because "other people touched them and you never know what bad luck they could have left on them."

Amulets are easier to make because they have one job: to repel what we don't want. Talismans require more thought, planning, care, and focus because we charge them with our desires.

Begin by choosing your amulet or talisman. Some symbols are very overt, such as a corno. Other symbols are far more discrete, like a sea horse pendant. What is most important is the object must resonate with you. What do I mean by resonate? It must ring true to who you are. You must genuinely love the shape of it, how it looks, and how it feels. Some believe that you must receive an amulet or a talisman as a gift for it to be effective. I don't feel this way, because I have both amulets and talismans I received as gifts and others I've purchased or made myself, and I don't find any difference. Whether you receive an amulet or a talisman as a gift, purchase it, or make it, the most important thing you need to do is cleanse or purify it of whatever energies it has absorbed prior to becoming yours.

There are many ways to cleanse or purify an amulet. The method of cleansing should be chosen primarily based on the material the amulet is made of. Consider items that can be immersed in water versus items that will be damaged by water. The ritual you use to cleanse and purify your amulet must resonate with you. Again, it is good to choose the method that feels most natural to you. Avoid rituals and practices that make you feel uncomfortable because this sensation of discomfort will distract from the purpose.

How I Cleanse an Amulet

I am a creature of both habit and tradition. I cleanse an amulet the way my zia taught me. In a bowl the right size, add fresh water, a squirt of dish soap, and a pinch of salt. Swish the amulet around in the water three times counterclockwise. Then pull it out, rinse under running water, and pat it dry with a clean dish cloth. If it still isn't dry, rest it on the cloth to finish air drying. Once it's dry, pick it up, say "Che mi porta fortuna" ("May it bring me luck"), and kiss it.

Use the same procedure with religious items—except at the end, say, "Saint____, che mi protegge/benedica" ("Saint_____, may they protect/bless me").

It is hard-coded in me to choose amulets made of materials that are not damaged by water; however, there are things that I don't want to chance in water. In this case, cleansing with just salt and a clean cloth will do. Take a bowl large enough to contain just enough salt to bury the item. Bury the item in the salt and leave it there for at least a half hour, or longer if you feel it's necessary. Dig it out and wipe the item in downward strokes with a clean cloth. Then say the words and kiss it, and it's all set to do its job.

One last thing: no one else should touch your amulet. If this happens or you suspect someone touched it, just repeat the cleansing. Do a cleansing of your amulets whenever you feel they need it. I usually do one if I haven't used an amulet in a long while. I go by how the object feels in my hand.

How to Make an Amulet into a Talisman

So, you've decided that you want to make an amulet into a special-purpose talisman. This process is a little more involved and requires care and attention because you are not just cleansing an amulet; you are charging a talisman with magic.

First, you need to choose the right amulet. As I stated earlier, there are many amulets (mine is not an exhaustive list), and these amulets pretty much serve the same purpose—to bring good luck or protect against bad luck. Any amulet will work, but you must choose the one that harmonizes with your intention for the talisman to be effective.

Choose an amulet that you identify with culturally. I'm not saying you cannot use an amulet of a different culture than your own. What I am saying is you need to feel a connection to the amulet of that culture. I have had remarkable success with amulets of different cultures, such as an Egyptian cartouche. The reason is that they were amuletic symbols intended for a specific purpose. (By the way, Egyptian cartouches are ancient, and even one purchased at a flea market can be outrageously powerful, provided the hieroglyphics are, in fact, the real symbols.)

It is best to choose an amulet for which you already feel an emotional attachment. For example, I feel strongly emotionally attached to my pewter pentacle pendant that I have had for decades. It is unique and looks and feels like "me." This bond between my pentacle and me enhances its power. I feel a similar bond with a garnet pendant I've also had for ages. It's nothing to look at. It looks like a nondescript lump. Yet, I have such a strong attachment to it that it is often the first amulet I reach for when I need comfort.

Lastly, you need to choose an amulet that inherently has properties that harmonize with your intention for the talisman. For example, when I use my garnet, I must make sure that I use it for purposes that are in line with the natural properties of garnet. A talisman need not be a pendant or piece of jewelry. It can be anything you wear or can carry with you discreetly.

Let's begin:

1. You have selected your amulet.

2. Cleanse your amulet with the method I described earlier.

3. Wear your amulet in specific situations.

   Let me explain step 3 better. Suppose you chose a bracelet as your amulet and wish to make it into a talisman for business negotiations because this is the line of work you are in. Wear it whenever you are participating in business negotiations. Wear it on your nondominant wrist. Then, whenever you experience success at work, no matter how small, touch your amulet with your dominant hand to charge the amulet with that successful energy.

4. Make a ritual of placing your dominant hand on your talisman and, with a clear mind, reliving a successful moment and imagining a future success you want to achieve.

5. Keep it simple. Don't overload your talisman with conflicting desires.

6. Do not share your talisman. You must never lend it or allow anyone else to wear or hold it unless you are giving or lending it to someone intentionally. That person really should cleanse it before using it, and you should cleanse it if it is returned to you. Cleansing does not completely remove the charge but does weaken it. Cleansing does remove all personal energy.

7. Anytime the energy of your talisman feels "muddled" or stale, simply cleanse it and go through these steps again.

A talisman becomes more powerful with repeated use.

How to Make a Standard Talisman for Protection against Magic and Malocchio

The following are instructions on how to make a commonly known (to those who know) talisman. This talisman can be as small as you like but does not need to be larger than one inch square. You want to be able to wear it discreetly pinned on the inside of your clothing.

<u>What You Will Need</u>

A small piece of fabric in a deep shade of red

Matching sewing thread

Scissors

Sewing needle

Small gold-colored safety pin

Small stone from a cemetery (if your ancestors are buried there, bonus!)

Coarse salt

3 wheat berries (optional)

1. Cut your fabric into a rectangle about one inch by two inches. Fold it in half with the right side of the fabric on the inside so you now have about a one-inch square.

2. With red thread, sew up the sides to make a pocket.

3. Now turn the pocket inside out so that the right side of the fabric is on the outside.

4. Place in it the stone, three grains of coarse (or a pinch of fine) salt, and three wheat berries if you have some.

5. Tuck the open end of the fabric in like you would a pillow-case over a pillow and sew it shut.

6. You're done. Use the safety pin to pin it to the inside of your clothing.

You don't need to cleanse this talisman, because you have placed salt inside it. Salt removes and repels all negative energy. Take care to remove the talisman from your clothing before washing. If you accidentally wash it, you can just open it up, replace the salt that may have dissolved in the wash, and close it back up, or make a new one.

Chapter 8

Communication
or Divination

Cartomancy

As far back as I can remember, I have always loved cards, all kinds of cards. When I was five, I was given a clear plastic case that contained six little decks of cards. Each deck was a card game: Animal Rummy, Authors, Snap, Old Maid, Hearts, and Crazy Eights. I played with these cards for hours on end. Each deck was beautifully illustrated. I came to know each deck intimately. The characters in each deck were my friends from another world, and I would spend hours visiting with them. Playing cards, such as the decks we play rummy or poker with, appealed to me with their black and red numbers, shapes, and faces on a stark, white background. I told stories to myself with these cards, assigning certain cards to the people in my life. I did the same thing with Italian playing cards. Playing with my cards was one of my favorite pastimes, along with reading and drawing.

One afternoon, I was playing with my Animal Rummy cards when a thought popped in my head, and I looked up and said, "We need to set another place at the table today because my uncle is coming over."

My zia paid no mind. This uncle lived hundreds of miles away. About forty-five minutes after I said it, the doorbell rang. It was my uncle! When he left, my zia became very angry with me. "Who told you he was coming? How did you know? Who have you been talking to?" I answered, "No one. I just thought it." My zia didn't believe me. She was angry with me, and I was punished for lying.

This lesson taught me to keep thoughts that popped in my head to myself. You must be wondering if I had read in the cards that my uncle was coming? No. No, I didn't. At the time, I didn't know how to read cards. I just played with them. The thing is, thoughts would pop in my head all the time, but especially when I played with my cards.

All forms of divination are viewed as communication and assessment tools. Cards, scrying, and dream interpretation are some examples of the tools we use to communicate with the other world and that the other world uses to communicate with us.

A common view is that cards are to be used to foresee the future. This is the least of what we can do with cards! They can do so much more than that. We can use them to assess the present. They are very helpful in the analysis of a situation in order to shed light on the motivations of everyone involved. This would apply to a new relationship or business venture or simply to see if things are, in fact, as they seem. Reading cards is considered active communication because we initiate the contact.

I learned to read Italian playing cards when I was seven. My first deck was a grimy old set held together with a rubber band that had been previously wrapped around broccoli rabe from the supermarket. This was the deck my family used to play *scopa*, an Italian card game.

That summer my dad took me to his hometown in Italy for the first time. A kind lady who had been best friends with my late paternal nonna sat down with me and taught me the meanings of each card. After that, I carried my deck and list of card meanings around everywhere.

Sometime later, a neighbor taught me how to reset or clean the cards, as we called it, and to only use my deck for reading. Cleaning the cards refreshes them and clears the deck of emotional imprints.

This is especially important when you've been handling your cards a lot during an emotionally trying time or when you just feel that they need a reset. It's important to do this with a brand-new deck as well.

It's been forty years since I first learned to read them, and I have to admit that I've never been able to memorize the meanings of the cards. What I mean is, I can't look at cards and know the meaning of each individual card. I use the cards as a focal point, and I rely on my experience and the patterns that trigger thoughts and messages to pop in my head. I compare reading them to learning to read sheet music to play an instrument versus learning to play an instrument by ear. I tell you this because I want you to be open-minded with how *you* will learn to read the cards. The magic is not inherent in the deck of cards. The magic is inherent in *you*, the practitioner. As with any other skill, some will have a natural talent and will pick it up in no time. Others will have to just work a little harder at it. Cards have always been my favorite game, and cartomancy (the art of reading cards) was my gateway into this magical world I live in, thus making it my favorite divination tool.

Well, then, let us get you started. Italian playing cards are widely available in all Italian grocery stores and online. So far I have been calling them Italian playing cards, but this is not entirely accurate. If you are familiar with Tarot de Marseilles, you will see the strong resemblance to the minor arcana. The interesting thing about Italian playing cards is that they are regional. The suits remain the same (swords, cups, clubs, coins), with decks named for a city or region. Northern Italian decks are French inspired, and therefore, the art style is very distinct from southern Italian decks of Spanish art style. They are all the same cards, but the art and style change based on the region or city in Italy they represent. So, if your family hails from Trieste, you may want a Triestine deck; if they hail from Treviso, you may want a Trevigiano deck, and so forth. Mine is a Neapolitan deck.

Care and Keeping of Cards

Obtain a brand-new deck or liberate one from your family home, I won't judge.

Begin by cleaning your cards. It is best to do this after a full moon, but before the new moon, so while the moon is waning or during the dark moon phase. My neighbor, who never went to church, warned to clean your cards only when the moon was not visible in the sky "so la Madonna doesn't see what we're doing, because it's disrespectful."

To do this, place all your cards in order. All decks consist of forty cards numbered ace to seven. Court cards consist of the Lady (*Dama*), Horse or Horseman (*Cavallo*), and King (*Re*). When you're playing card games, the Lady is equivalent to eight, the Horseman nine, and the King is ten. Therefore, you place the cards in this order: ace, two, three, four, five, six, seven, Lady, Horseman, King.

Once your cards are in numerical order and divided into suits, stack your suits from the bottom up in this order: *spade* (spa-deh = swords), *denari* (de-nah-ree = coins), *bastone* (ba-sto-neh = clubs), and lastly at the top of your deck, *coppe* (coh-ppeh = cups). Now take your deck and place it in a bowl. The bowl has to be large enough to bury your deck in salt. The salt serves two functions. The first is to clear the cards of unwanted energies. The second is to "magnetize" them so that they absorb your energy. I use inexpensive table salt that I reuse every time I clean my cards. Cover the bowl with a napkin and lay it to rest somewhere it will not be disturbed for three days and three nights. Once the time has passed, take your deck out of the bowl and wipe your cards with a clean cloth. Your cards are now reset and ready to use. Store your cards in a dedicated box or bag.

Card Meanings

Each card is interpreted in relation to the adjacent card(s) in the spread. The reader studies the layout and then interprets the cards based on the entire picture. It takes a lot of practice and many readings to learn to read the patterns and their meanings. I'm not going to tell you that learning to read them won't be frustrating. It will be so frustrating that you will want to give up. Don't. I promise you that your hard work and perseverance will pay off. One day it will all coalesce, and in that moment, the magic will happen and suddenly you will "get it" and it will be fantastic!

In my humble opinion, Italian playing cards are the best for detailed readings that seamlessly blend day-to-day mundanities and the arcane. In these cards, you can read whether the business deal you are entering is in your best interest and whether your mother-in-law has placed a curse on you. All in the same layout. That's right.

Coppe/Cups

ASSO/ACE: Home, family, family and financial stability, manifestation, joy.

2: Falling in love, attraction, new relationship, early stage of a love relationship, joy.

3: Long-term relationship, healthy relationship, attainment, reward, gift, joy.

4: Distrust, strained relationships, stalemate, confirmed suspicion.

5: Pregnancy, birth, joy, abundance.

6: Regarding love: worry, doubts, insecurity, jealousy, a fling.

7: Newfound happiness, comfort, happy relationship, true love, party or celebration.

DAMA/LADY: Woman with fair hair, a good woman, a marriage proposal.

CAVALLO/HORSEMAN: Young man, sexy, seductive and intelligent man, courtship, lovemaking, powerful friends.

RE/KING: Man, kind, loving, generous, sincere. Truth.

Bastoni/Clubs

ASSO/ACE: Triumph, vitality, virility, enchantment, magic.

2: Misunderstanding, disagreement, argument, escape, malaise.

3: Strong relationship or business partnership.

4: Quarrel, adversity, malaise, heartbreak, long illness.

5: Moodiness, worry, anxiety, clandestine meeting, last will and testament, prison sentence.

6: Quarrel, complication, falsehood, slander.

7: Certification, completed transaction, stability.

DAMA/LADY: Woman, kind and faithful. Also a trip, train station, market square.

CAVALLO/HORSEMAN: Young man, kind, affectionate, and intelligent.

RE/KING: Man, patient, kind, and hardworking. Also, place of work like an office or store.

Denari/Coins

ASSO/ACE: A large amount of money. Luck. Change of fortune.

2: Meeting, wedding engagement, peace, lasting agreement.

3: Good business deal, luck at gambling, out-of-control spending.

4: Financial loss, failure, fraud, deception, bankruptcy.

5: Communication, letter, happy news.

6: Sorrow, solitude, loneliness, grief, financial loss, bad decision.

7: Love letter, money, luck, financial gain.

DAMA/LADY: Woman, false rival. Also a pact, commitment, contract.

CAVALLO/HORSEMAN: Man, sly, gambler. Also: winnings, gains, bank.

RE/KING: Business man, speculator, cunning. Money, refund, safe such as in vault.

Spade/Swords

ASSO/ACE: Positive: Good news, surprise. Negative: Affliction. Anxiety, stabbed in the heart (heartbreak, betrayal).

2: Breakup, quitting, abandonment.

3: Quarrel, complication, falsehood, slander, verbal abuse.

4: Heartbreak, illness, danger, accident, injury, problems, conflict.

5: Regret, remorse.

6: Pain, brief illness, obstacle, blockage.

7: Vacation, trip, love affair, sad goodbyes, escapism.

DAMA/LADY: Evil woman, witch. Separation, court proceedings.

CAVALLO/HORSEMAN: A man in uniform/suit. Harassment, misunderstanding.

RE/KING: A difficult and mean man. An evil man. Enemy. Isolation and loneliness.

How to Start

I will share what I do, but you may want to do it differently. It has to be what works for you.

I was taught to recite an incantation before reading cards. I've heard a number of versions. They pretty much all ask for the same thing. Here is one:

"Carte, cartina, scopra le vie e non dire bugie!"

This translates to invoking the "cards, (and) map (in reference to the layout), show the way and do not lie!"

To be honest, repeating this incantation is not me, so I say nothing. I feel more comfortable saying a silent prayer to my ancestors and spirit guides to help me see the matter clearly.

The Method

A typical reading ranges anywhere from nine to fifteen cards in total. If you already have a layout you feel comfortable with—for example, The Celtic Cross—go ahead and use it. My experience has been that I have to be comfortable with the layout. If I'm comfortable with the layout, the rest falls into place. Here is the method I use to read the cards. It is very simple. First, shuffle the cards, ask the person for whom you are reading to cut the deck in two or three with their left hand, and then pick up the deck and lay the cards down on the table three by three for a total of nine cards. The first row of three cards represents the matter at hand. The second row of three cards represents factors influencing the matter at hand. The last row of three cards represents actions we need to take, if any, and the outcome. If the nine cards on the table do not contain enough information, as is sometimes the case for the second and sometimes the third row of cards, I pick another and then another for a maximum total of fifteen cards. This same nine-card method is helpful for dream interpretation as well. In the case of dream interpretation, the first row of three cards represents the matter that the dream is addressing. The second row represents the message ancestors or spirits are trying to convey through the dream. The third row of three cards represents actions we need to take, if any, and the outcome.

Dreams

From an early age, I was taught to remember my dreams and look for messages. In my family as well as in my Italian community, it seemed that every conversation included a discussion surrounding dreams. If someone was going through a tough time, we would invariably ask, "How are you feeling today? What (or who) did you dream last night?"

Dreams and omens are considered passive communication because it is the spirit world that initiates contact. When I talk about dreams, I don't just mean remembering your dreams and then looking them up in a dream dictionary. Don't get me wrong; this is a great way to begin to explore your dreams, but what I am talking about is developing a relationship with your dream space. The more developed your relationship is, the more adept you will become at accessing it.

First, you need to explore what your dreams mean to you right now. Maybe you never gave them much thought. Maybe you don't remember your dreams. Perhaps like me you've studied psychology and view your dreams as your subconscious working things out. It doesn't matter what they mean to you right now; what matters is that you determine what that meaning is, because it is your starting point.

Whether you remember your dreams or not, your dream space is where most of your spiritual communication and magic occur. The reason is that your dream space exists outside of time. The most important are the moment just before you fall asleep and the moment just before you wake up. This is a liminal place, and thus, it is where your spirit can meet up and visit with spirits from the other world.

To develop a strong connection with your dream space, you must begin by practicing good sleep hygiene. Sleep patterns do not affect only your waking hours.

If you do not have a bedtime routine already, you need to make one because you will then incorporate your sleep ritual into your bedtime routine.

To give you an idea of a routine, this is what mine looks like at the moment:

1. Walk my dog.

2. Make a cup of tea.

3. Get ready for bed.

4. Write down anything that may be troubling me, concerns, and/or questions in my dream journal that I keep in my bedside table.

5. If I want to dream of a specific person, I ask that person to come visit me using something that reminds me of them and makes me feel like they are present. I do this by preparing a special meal I identify with them, wearing a piece of jewelry, or surrounding myself with a scent I associate with them. For example, if I wish to dream of my late mom, I dab on some White Lavender by Yardley, a perfume she wore when I was a child.

6. Drink my tea and go to bed.

In the morning, the first thing I do is try to remember my dreams and write about them in my journal before they leave me. Some mornings I am able to write a paragraph. Other times a word or two. There are times when I cannot articulate in words, so I draw a picture. If I don't remember my dreams, I write in my journal how I feel upon awaking. Then, I go on with my day.

Like everything else worth doing, this process takes effort, consistency, and patience. At the start, it may seem that you are not remembering your dreams or that maybe you aren't dreaming at all. Rest assured, something is going on. You just don't see it yet. When I am worried about something, I write it in my dream journal and promptly forget about it. Sometimes that is all you need to move on from a worry that has been taking up all your energy. You may not dream anything at all about it, BUT the worry has magically left you. This is a gift. Make sure to say your thanks.

Other times, you may find that you are having vivid, even wacky dreams. Write down whatever you remember, no matter how bizarre, nonsensical, or just plain disconnected it may appear. Use words, drawings, colors, a song you may have on your mind upon awaking, a scent, or whatever comes to mind. Over time you will see that your dream space has a language all its own. You will see the connection between certain dreams and things happening in your waking hours. This is beyond the scope of a dream dictionary. This journal will become your personal dream lexicon. It will literally become the medium by which you communicate with ancestors and spirits regarding all things. Don't feel discouraged if at first it seems like nothing is going on; just keep at it. I promise, it will come.

Although my goal is not to write a dream dictionary, I did want to share with you some common dreams and meanings I was taught when I was very young and that have remained with me my entire life. You may find these are true for you to some degree, or not. The whole point of the dream journal is to learn the language of *your* dream life.

Blood: Blood represents happiness; joy commensurate with the amount of blood.

Bread: Bread means abundance; you will always have enough to eat.

Bride not wearing white: This means the relationship is solid.

Bride wearing white: This indicates a breakup.

Cat: If you see a cat in your dreams, right away my zia would blurt out: "betrayal from someone you trust." This meaning is universal among Italians. However, it can also indicate your need for independence or freedom, usually relating to responsibilities. My experience has been that when I dream of a cat, although in my dream I am thinking, "Oh great, a betrayal" (this thinking is hard-coded!), more often than not, when I wake, I realize there is drama around me and the cat in my dream is my desire to not become sucked into it and to remain aloof.

Child: If you see a child, you will have a disagreement with someone.

Clothing: This means someone has cast or is attempting to cast a spell on you.

Death: If someone dies in your dream, that adds seven years to their lives.

Dog: Typically, a dog in your dream means loyalty. However, the dog may simply be a spirit guide. It could be guarding you to keep you safe, comforting you because you are sad or grieving, or visiting you because your dog has died. My dogs visit me when I am missing them or whenever I need to be comforted.

Driving: This means someone is trying to control you.

Earth or soil: This means you need to pay attention to your affairs of this world.

Famous people: If you interact with famous people, fame is your destiny.

Father: Dreaming of your father represents security. You will always be taken care of.

Feces: This means unexpected money commensurate to the amount of feces in your dream.

Fire: If you see fire in your dreams, you will learn a truth that someone is expending a lot of energy to conceal.

Funeral: A funeral means you have unfinished business.

Hair: Hair falling out means you will experience a loss. If it is ruined by someone else, someone is jealous of you. This is also a symptom of malocchio (the evil eye). Do not get your hair done. You will be bitterly disappointed with the result. Make sure to have the malocchio removed immediately.

Infant: This dream means you will have a terrible argument with someone close to you or break up.

Insect: An insect means a small temporary or chronic illness.

Mother: A dream about your mother is a spiritual dream. It means you are loved unconditionally.

Naked: If you're naked in your dreams, your enemies are plotting to expose you!

People you don't know: If you see people you don't know, they may be ancestors you have never met or angels guiding you. They may come to you as completely unknown people or fictitious characters from books, TV, movies, and so forth.

People you know: If you see people you know, you are visiting with each other in the dream space.

Reception hall: A reception hall represents the afterlife. That is where we visit our deceased loved ones. Typically, we dream of newly deceased loved ones in a party hall setting. This is how they inform us they have arrived safely.

Restaurant: A restaurant also represents the afterlife. This is a more intimate setting than the reception hall, however. This is where we meet up with deceased loved ones. The reason we meet them in this more intimate setting is that we asked them to promise they will visit us after they die and they promised they would. When my father was dying of brain cancer, I asked him whether he would visit me. We had a very complicated relationship. On his deathbed, he vowed that he definitely would visit, if he could. Many months later, I did dream I met my father for lunch in a little restaurant. He looked healthy, happy, and handsome. He was impeccably dressed, as he was in life, and as if he never had cancer.

Snake: This means a health scare.

Spider: A spider represents wealth. It's a good omen for business deals.

Table: This is a curse. If you dream you are sitting at a table and your attention is focused on the table, look at who else is there with you. This dream means the people you break bread with wish you harm. In the extreme, it means someone has placed a *fattura* (curse) on you.

Teeth: If you dream that your teeth are falling out, it means news of a death.

Urine: This represents loss of money, such as a poor investment or unexpected bills.

Water: Water means a you are going through a very emotional time.

Wedding: Dreaming about a wedding means you will be attending a funeral.

Woman (blonde hair): She represents bad luck. Someone is working black magic against you. Curse.

Wedding Band and Water Pendulum

Another method of divination close to my heart is the wedding band pendulum. I learned of this method in my teens from one of my friends. I have the fondest memories of Saturday nights with my friends when we would borrow a friend's mom's wedding band, slip it onto kitchen string, and suspend it over a tall glass of water almost filled to the top. Enough room has to be left so the ring is completely in the glass. The ring has to be a plain circle and blessed by a priest (hence the wedding band), and the ring must only barely skim the surface of the water.

This method works well only for close-ended questions that can be answered with a "yes" or "no" and counting questions, where the number of ring hits against the glass can add up to a number, days, letters of the alphabet, etc.

Procedure

With your elbows on the table, hold the ring pendulum steady, until it barely touches the surface of the water. The ring will begin to swing back and forth. You count only the swings whereby the ring actually hits the glass, making a distinct "ding" sound.

One ding for Yes.

Two dings for No.

You may also ask questions regarding time, such as "In how many years, days, weeks, months, or years will something happen?"

Ask your question: "In how many . . . ?" Then count the number of times the ring hits the glass.

Another variation is using a pendulum to predict the sex of a child. In this method, you hold a gold chain necklace (this was used because literally everyone wore one when I was growing up) over the pregnant belly of the expectant mother. If the chain swings in a circle, it's a girl. If the chain swings back and forth in a straight line, it's a boy.

Favomancy

I didn't realize favomancy was a real thing and had a name until I was in my twenties. I thought it was a time-waster taught to me when I was little to make shelling bushels of Romano, kidney, and fava beans less tedious. I assure you, shelling bushels of beans every September is tedious no matter what.

Favomancy really is pretty much like reading the symbols in tea leaves or Turkish coffee. The object is to scatter the beans and interpret the shape formed or created on the surface where they land.

This really wasn't my favorite form of divination, although one of my neighbors swore her late mother sent her messages through the beans. Her beans of choice were coffee beans. She would take a handful of coffee beans and toss them on a clean, white cotton cloth, read them, and then grind them up and drink them.

I never really warmed up to favomancy because, well, I was shelling beans for days!

Reading Water

Water and oil are also used to diagnose malocchio.

Oil added to a white, shallow bowl two-thirds filled with water is the method most commonly used (in conjunction with the assessment of other symptoms) to read if someone is afflicted with malocchio.

What You Will Need

A white, shallow bowl

Water

Olive oil

Teaspoon

Fill the bowl two-thirds of the way with fresh water. Pour olive oil onto a teaspoon. Add three drops of oil into the water from the spoon.

» If the drops remain intact in the water, there is no malocchio.

» If the drops of oil burst and disappear in the water, there is malocchio present and it must be removed.

Water and Wine to Check for Fatture (Spells, Curses)

As with malocchio, there are signs and symptoms that indicate fatture (plural: curses). Once a practitioner suspects the presence of a fattura (singular: a curse), a water and wine test is done to confirm it.

What You Will Need

1-quart glass jar with a tight-fitting lid

2 cups water

1 fluid ounce robust red wine such as Chianti, Merlot, or homemade

Fill your glass jar halfway with two cups of water. Now pour in one fluid ounce (thirty milliliters) of a robust red wine. Place the lid tightly on the jar and set it to rest in a dark place where you know it will not be disturbed. Wait twenty-four hours. Now check your jar. If it looks like it did when you placed it in the cupboard, clear and easy to see through, even if the wine has separated from the water, the test is negative for a fattura. If instead you find that the wine has coagulated or turned the entire contents of the jar opaque, the test is positive for fattura.

My father would experience the most vivid nightmares. Every time he did, he would perform this simple test to make sure someone hadn't placed a curse on him. I remember asking him: "How is it possible for wine to coagulate in plain water?" In his characteristic Italian American accent, he would reply, quite impatiently: "Ma what-a you no undastend now? It's-a not-a science, Mary-Grace, it's-a paranormal."

Book Oracle

Another form of divination is using a favorite or meaningful book, a book that speaks to you as an oracle. This technique is used very much in the same manner you would use tarot cards.

My zia used her worn copy of *La Sacra Bibbia* (The Holy Bible), and my dad preferred to use his favorite book, *La Divina Commedia* (*The Divine Comedy*) by Dante Alighieri. This practice was as natural to my zia and dad as brushing their teeth. When I pointed out to my devoutly Catholic zia that using her Sacra Bibbia in this manner was the same as using cards, she would get quite defensive! My dad, on the other hand, would say: "Dante understands me and speaks to my soul."

I've used both of these books and some others with surprisingly and consistently accurate results. I recommend you try this form of divination with a book that is very meaningful to you. If the book already speaks to you, using it in this manner will make it exponentially so.

How do you use a book as an oracle?

Meditate on your situation, concern, or question while holding your book in your hands. When you are ready, open your book randomly. Look down and the first thing you read is your message in response to your question. Sometimes the message is a metaphor. Other times, the message can be read at face value. For an example right here and right now, I just walked over to my bookshelf and selected a book at random. The book was *Papa, My Father* by Leo Buscaglia. Surprisingly, I didn't have anything I was currently worried about. So, for this example, I asked this question: "Do you have a message for me?" (Excuse me while I consult the book.)

First, I thought about this question and then opened the book to a random page. I opened the book, and it landed on a mostly blank page with only this quote on it:

> To show a child what has once delighted you, to find the child's delight added to your own, so that there is now a double delight seen in the glow of trust and affection. This is happiness.
>
> —J. B. Priestly

I can imagine that, to you, both my question and this answer seem pretty random. To me, the answer resonated deep in my soul because this is why I am writing this book.

It may take a little time to get the hang of this technique. You can take your book with you anywhere you go. You can easily consult your inconspicuous oracle in plain view anywhere you may be, with no one being the wiser.

Tarocchi (Tarot)

Ruggiero (whose name is changed to protect his identity) was an old family friend from Naples. He was a physically imposing man with olive skin, jet black hair, and emerald green eyes. Ruggiero was easy to talk to, with a dry sense of humor and a quick wit; he was incredibly magnetic and funny. Underneath this master of ceremonies type façade was a spiritual (but not religious), mystical man who lived and breathed magic. Although I was introduced to him as Grace, he called me Raziel [pronounced RAH-tzee-ehl], a commonly used diminutive of Graziella, which is Gracey in Italian. Ruggiero adored me from the moment we met.

"Do you know that there is an archangel of the Kabbalah assigned to the keeping of mysteries and secrets named Raziel?" he asked me. "No, I didn't." "How apropos," he replied with twinkling green eyes. Over the course of the next year, he would make sure to bring up the archangel Raziel whenever he introduced me to someone new. Most times it was a lighthearted flourish added to the introduction. Other times, there would be just a barely detectable threat in his tone.

Ruggiero loved i tarocchi and was convinced that, with my help, he would crack the code to the winning lotto numbers. In exchange for my visiting him with my tarot deck, he taught me how to use tarot for spellcasting. This was much to my colleague's amusement. Coincidentally, Ruggiero was a patient on the hospital ward where I was working following his fall from a scaffold that resulted in a broken neck. Long recovery time meant he was there for a several months.

At the end of shift and sometimes my day off, we would sit and visit in a cheerful sunroom. I brought my tarot deck, and Ruggiero would pick thirteen from the seventy-eight cards spread out and facedown. We studied each card for symbols and numbers and discussed it until every possible number was extracted from it. Ruggiero would then prep his lotto card and hand it to his son, Franco, who visited him daily to pick up his tickets. This Wednesday evening routine went on for several months. I enjoyed my visits with Ruggiero. Our card reading made him tremendously happy, and it pleased his son to see his father happy. As long as Franco's father was happy, all was right in his world.

One evening in late August, I was at Ruggiero's house. I had accompanied my aunt, who wanted to visit with Ruggiero's wife, Carmela. The phone rang and Carmela went to answer it. I could hear Carmela, on the phone saying: "Rugge, please, slow down, I can't make out what you are saying. Why are you so worked up? What are you saying did I check the lotto ticket to—," and then, silence. Carmela, looking like she saw a ghost, handed me the phone. "Hello?"

"Raziel! I want you to go to the car dealership across the street and pick out something nice to replace that rust bucket you call a car."

"Ruggiero, what are you saying?" I asked.

"Six out of six numbers. One million bananas. You did it, baby! The tarocchi came through!"

Not once had it ever occurred to me to pick up a lotto ticket of my own. To be truthful, I didn't really believe it would work.

"Are you telling me you won the lotto for real?" and just as I said it, I looked up to see his son, Franco, walk into the living room. He stood there, fixing me with a deer-in-headlights look, white as a ghost, and a cigarette dangling from his lips dropped to the floor. The house was so quiet, so still, that the cigarette appeared to make a loud thump when it landed on the ceramic tile.

Franco picked the cigarette off the floor and slowly walked toward me. I handed him the phone.

"Allo, Pa? Wait a second. Listen to me, Pa. Are you listening to me? I need to tell you something. Are you listening? I didn't play your numbers this week. I forgot."

Dead silence followed for what seemed an eternity, and then I could hear Ruggiero's voice loud and clear from the phone across the room: "I swear to God and all there is, son or no son, I'm going to kill you when I get out!"

With that, my aunt and I thanked Carmela for the visit and coffee and quickly took our leave.

Using Tarocchi (Tarot) to Divine Lottery Numbers

I know what you're thinking. You are wondering whether I have personally used this method to divine lotto numbers for myself. I have. For ten years now, I have been playing the same numbers I used the tarot to pick. Occasionally, I win a free ticket here and seventy-five dollars there. I haven't scored the big one yet! My wish for you is that you have better luck!

What You Will Need

Time. For real, this takes quite a lot of time at the start. Keep
your notes so you don't have to analyze the same card more
than once.

Tarot deck. (I use a Rider-Waite deck for this purpose.)

Notepad dedicated specifically to lotto numbers. Keep a record
of all the numbers so you can spot patterns and trends.

Pen or pencil.

Shuffle your tarot deck, and when you are ready, spread the cards out
facedown on a table.

With your nondominant hand, select thirteen cards. Put the
remaining cards away. One by one, go through each card looking for
any kind of number clue. Look for anything from the obvious number, such as the number at the top of the card, to the number of, say,
clouds. For example, I picked the Queen of Swords at random from
my deck just now. Here is the analysis:

Always start by writing the date at the top of the page.

Queen of Swords

1: woman, sword, angel, bird, crown, throne, etc.

4: trees

5: butterflies

13: clouds surrounding the queen

32: clouds on her cape

. . . and so on until you are done finding things to count.

Repeat the exact same thing with the remaining twelve cards.

Once done, look at the overall picture. This system will provide
you with a wealth of numbers to play. Does a number appear over
and over again? Make sure to play that number. If, for instance, that
number is 4 and it appears ten times, play 4, 10, 40, etc.

Buona fortuna! Good luck!

Using Tarot for Spellcasting

I must begin by saying that I've never felt truly comfortable with this method for a couple of reasons, at least. The first is that you really do need an expert level in tarot interpretation to carry out this type of spellcasting safely. I have never felt confident that I had that level of expertise. The second reason is that I have seen it work, and fast. However, I have also seen results that were wildly unpredictable and out of control. These unpredictable and out-of-control results were directly the fault of not having a thorough understanding of tarot symbolism. Another reason I've never felt comfortable with this method is that when I asked my teacher how to undo the spell for whatever reason, his reply was: "You can't. There is no undoing. The story as you wrote it has been sent into the ether and it must now unfold. If you then decide you've changed your mind or made a mistake, you may have to wait until your spell has run its course and cast a new one."

Now for the procedure.

What you are basically doing is a tarot reading in reverse . . . kind of. You are creating a storyboard or graphic novel with tarot cards to tell the story of the reality you intend to create.

What You Will Need

Tarot deck (I will be using Rider-Waite in my example.)

A notebook dedicated to spellcasting, or a sheet of paper

Pen/pencil

Here's an example: Suppose you desire to go overseas in search of gainful employment.

Pick out a tarot card to represent you. I am a Leo woman, and thus, I would pick the Queen of Wands.

Now the rest: Six of Swords, Two of Pentacles, Eight of Pentacles, Nine of Pentacles.

The old method was to write down these cards in a notebook followed by drawing it like a graphic novel. Nowadays with smartphones and tablets, you can simply line up your cards, take a picture, and store it in a folder on your electronic device. I don't know if this method will be just as effective. I'm more old school when it comes to these things. I truly believe that the magic is the meditation and intention inherent in literally and deliberately drawing the story you want to unfold.

Now suppose the universe suddenly aligns and you find yourself faced with all the correct circumstances. You've just received a lucrative job offer overseas—even better than the spell you cast! But suppose you've changed your mind and don't want to leave? Maybe you've lost your taste for what you thought you wanted. Then do what you want to do. Stay. Nothing bad will happen. That's because, in my example, you aren't attempting to control or harm anyone.

Chapter 9

Spells and Charms

When it comes to magic, the most important thing after intent is timing. Working when the moon is right for your specific goal will give the best results. To create or bring a condition into your life (such as love), cast your spell starting on a new moon when it is waxing. To rid yourself of a condition such as an illness, cast your spell anytime from the day after the moon is fullest when it is waning. Gratitude rituals are carried out when the moon is full.

Days of the Week

Sunday

Sunday is ruled by the sun and the Roman god Sol.
Cast spells related to success, ambition, career, healing.
Zodiac sign: Leo.
Color: yellow.
Metal: gold.
Element: fire.
Saints: all angels and saints.

Monday

Monday is ruled by the moon (Luna).

Roman moon goddesses: Diana and Juno.

Cast spells for psychic powers, clairvoyance, family matters, child-birth, and feminine concerns.

Zodiac sign: Cancer, Pisces.

Color: white.

Metal: silver.

Element: water.

Saints: The Holy Trinity, all female saints.

Tuesday

Tuesday is ruled by the planet Mars and the Roman god Mars.

Cast spells for courage and inner strength, men, sex, sexual potency, war, psychic defense, banishing, binding, curses, and hex breaking.

Zodiac signs: Aries, Scorpio.

Color: red.

Metal: iron.

Element: fire.

Saints: all angels and archangels, such as Saint Michael and Saint George.

Wednesday

Wednesday is ruled by the planet Mercury and the Roman god Mercury.

Cast spells for communication, education, creativity, travel, mental agility, writing, and art.

Zodiac signs: Gemini, Virgo.

Colors: green and red.

Metal: mercury.

Element: air.

Saints: Saint Joseph, Saints Peter and Paul, all Holy Apostles.

Thursday

Thursday is ruled by the planet Jupiter and the Roman god Jupiter/Jove.

Cast spells for wealth and expansion, political power, legal affairs, business, and insurance matters.

Zodiac sign: Sagittarius.

Color: sky blue.

Metal: tin.

Element: fire.

Saints: The Holy Spirit, The Blessed Sacrament, Jesus Christ.

Friday

Friday is ruled by the planet Venus and the Roman goddess Venus.

Cast spells for love, beauty, fertility and in celebration of nature.

Zodiac signs: Taurus, Libra.

Color: green.

Metals: copper and brass.

Element: earth.

Saints: Saint Gerard, Holy Cross, Sacred Heart of Jesus.

Saturday

Saturday is ruled by the planet Saturn and the Roman god Saturn.

Cast spells related to challenges that we meet in life to learn about ourselves. It's also a good day for working on property, inheritance, and agriculture.

Zodiac signs: Capricorn, Aquarius.

Color: black.

Metal: lead.

Element: earth.

Saints: all aspects of Mary.

Colors for Spell Working

This color guide is useful when choosing the correct color for candles, clothing, cloth for charm bags, and so on.

Black

Black is the complete absence of light. Black is used when the goal is to absorb light. Black can be used in hexing. People who work with energy and magic are drawn to wearing black because it absorbs light (all colors of the spectrum) and thus recharges them (chakras, aura, astral body). Black clothing also protects from psychic vampires, who are people who unknowingly (or knowingly) recharge themselves by plugging into other people and drain them of their light. You can tell you have been in the presence of a psychic vampire if you feel exhausted and drained after spending time with them.

Blue

Blue is the color of healing (mind and body), clarity, truth, self-expression, written communication, and travel.

Brown

Brown is a combination of red (masculine) and green (feminine). Use when you want to invoke balance, grounding, harmony, peaceful home, fertility, and healing for people and animals.

Green

Green is a combination of blue (inspiration) and yellow (creativity). Green is the color of choice for working on abundance, creativity, love, fertility, and luck.

Orange

Orange is a combination of red (power) and yellow (creativity). Use it when you are looking for strength, courage, luck, power, and justice.

Pink

Pink is a combination of red for passion and white for purity/innocence. Pink is the color of choice when invoking romantic love.

Red

Red is used primarily for psychic self-defense, such as a ward against malocchio and fattura. Use it to invoke lust, sexual energy, inner strength, and courage.

Violet

Violet is blue with a touch of red. Use it for spiritual healing, psychic abilities, magic, and wisdom.

White

White contains all colors of the spectrum. Use it when you want to reflect light or illuminate. It is used to invoke peace, purity, and purification. White also can be used in the place of any color in your magical workings.

Yellow/Gold

Yellow or gold is the color of joy, learning, creativity, imagination, communication, the mind, and friendship.

Supplies for Spell Working

Blessing: Sea salt, sugar, *acqua di colonia* (cologne water)

Cleansing: Cinnamon, lemon, sea salt, rosemary, rue

Fertility: Almond, *amaretti* (almond cookies), confetti (sugar-coated almonds), figs, honey, mustard, peaches, pears, poppy seeds

Happiness: Bergamot, cacao butter, celandine, hawthorn, hyacinth, mandarin, marjoram, orange

Healing: Coriander, garlic, juniper, knotweed, lavender, lemon, lemon and lime leaves, mallow, mint, nutmeg, rosemary, rue, sambuca (elderberry), tea

Love: Apple, basil, dill, honey, jasmine, lavender, lemon, rose

Prosperity: Allspice, anise, coffee, cinnamon, dried beans, grape, ginger, hazelnut, olive, walnut, wheat, wine

Protection: Bay, bistort (snakeweed), black pepper, chili pepper, cinnamon, clove, fennel, garlic, lavender, onion, orris, palm, pine, rue, Saint-John's-wort, spikenard, thyme, wheatberries, witch hazel

Sexual Attraction: Coconut, damiana, patchouli, cacao, cinnamon, clove, vanilla

Liquids

Alcohol:
Spirito pure alcohol.

Cologne:
Acqua di colonia (cologne water). This is a citrus-based cologne. One example is Florida Water. It is widely available in North America. A very old cologne from Germany, 4711, also does the trick. Both are used in cleansing and protection.

Liqueur:

Centerba Toro. This Italian liqueur from Tocco da Casauria, Abruzzo, is made from one hundred herbs. *Centerba* literally means one hundred herbs. It is used as a tonic for cleansing, protection, health, and hex breaking.

Liquore Amaretto. This Italian liqueur made from almonds is used for fertility.

Liquore Strega. This Italian liqueur from Benevento in the region of Campania is made from herbs. It is used for blessing (tonic), celebration, divination, and offering.

Oil:

Holy oil. It is used for healing and blessing.

Olive oil. This is my staple oil. I use it for all my work.

Vinegar:

Aceto Quattro ladri (Four Thieves Vinegar). This is an infusion of medicinal plants in vinegar (red, white, cider, or distilled wine), which was believed to have the power to protect from plague contagion. Placed in a spray bottle, it is used to physically clean and spiritually cleanse a surface.

Wine vinegar. It is used for cleansing and purification.

Water:

Holy water. It is used for blessing, cleansing, and protection.

Rose water. It is used for love and blessing.

Sea water. It is used for cleansing the body of stress and negative energy.

Spring water. It is used for cleansing objects. It is mixed with the listed liqueurs in the making of tonics.

Well water. It is used for cleansing objects. It is mixed with the listed liqueurs in the making of tonics.

Tools of the Trade

Amulets

Animalia: animal statues/figurines

Black string or ribbon

Book of Novenas

Book of Psalms

Bowl

Candles

Enamel or stainless steel pot

Fabric: small scraps of solid colors

Holy Bible—preferably the Douay-Rheims translation

Incense

Italian playing cards (reserved only for divination)

Knife

Mortar and pestle

Red string or ribbon

Roman goddesses/gods: pictures, statues, prayer cards

Rosary beads

Saints: pictures, statues, prayer cards, medals

Scissors

Sewing needles

Thread—a variety of colors

Various sacramentals

Wax

White string or ribbon

Wooden spoon

Spells and Charms

Health

The purpose of this spell is to maintain good health (also to protect from lightning strikes and storms). This ancient well-known prayer was used among Italian elders from a number of different regions. To obtain this blessing, recite this prayer outdoors first thing in the morning:

Pater Noster dei Sanctorum.

Maria bella angelorum.

Maria bella che dormiva, il figlio in sogno le appariva.

"Caro io ti ho sognato che al Calvario ti han portato. Coron d'oro t'han levato e le spine t'han piantato".

"Quel che dici è verità", rispose Cristo alla mammà.

Chi questo dice tre volte per via, paura non ha di alcune malattia.

Chi questo dice per tre volte in un campo, non ha paura di acqua, tuoni e lampo.

Our Father of saints.

Beautiful angel Mary.

Beautiful Mary was sleeping, and her son appeared in her dream.

"Dear one, I dreamt they took you to Calvary; they removed your gold crown and stuck you with thorns."

"What you say is truth," replied Christ to his mother.

He/She who recites these three times on the street fears not any illness.

He/She who recites these three times in a field fears not rain, thunder, and lightning.

San Cosimo e Damiano

Saints Cosmas and Damian were twin brothers and physicians. They are protectors of babies and young children. In olden days, mothers invoked them to heal their babies of intestinal worms (pinworms). Nowadays, we have medicine to treat intestinal parasites. This incantation serves two purposes: one physical (to drive out parasites such as pinworms) and the other metaphysical (to drive out parasites such as evil spirits).

The child's mother strokes the baby's belly clockwise with her right hand while reciting this prayer:

San Cosma e Damiano siete medico sovrano,

medico di Dio salvate _____ dai vermi,

questo verme che vuole il budello,

strappateglielo voi,

e tutto sminuzzato nelle feci va mandato.

Saints Cosmas and Damian, you are the supreme doctors,

doctors of God, save _____ from worms,

This worm that wants this intestine,

Tear it and crumble it up to be sent out through the feces.

Once the child's symptoms have passed, the mother recites the incantation again but this time adds a *Pater Noster* (Lord's Prayer) and a *Gloria* (Glory Be), in gratitude and as a seal to further protect the child from evil.

Love

To Know Your Future Husband

This novena to San Giovanni (Saint John the Baptist) is of Neapolitan origin. This ancient spell involves molten lead dropped in cold holy water and, once cooled, the shape was interpreted on the morning of June 24 to give a clue of the trade and financial standing of a young girl's future husband. The following is a modified spell that uses wax (ceromancy) instead of lead.

The novena to San Giovanni begins the evening of June 15 after the sun has set. The young lady stands outdoors in front of her home or on a balcony and recites the following every night, for nine nights (*novena* means a set of nine) until and including the night of June 23:

San Giovanni Benedetto,

pe' un infame maladetto,

foste a morte condannato,

con sto' piombo, coagulato,

conoscere mi fai,

la fortuna che mi dai,

San Giovanni della vita.

Blessed Saint John (the Baptist),

Due to the infamous and damned (King Herod),

You were sentenced to death,

With this coagulated lead (wax),

Reveal to me,

My life's fortune (destiny) that you grant me,

Saint John (the Baptist).

On the final night (June 23), a chunk of wax is melted in a pan and, once it is liquid, is poured into a bowl of cold holy water. The bowl is placed on the young lady's bedside table to inspire her to dream of her future husband. On the morning of June 24, the young lady reports on her dreams, and a married woman close to her interprets her dreams and the shape of the wax in the bowl to determine who her future husband will be, including his trade and financial/social standing.

To Win a Lottery

The goddess Fortuna is invoked to win a lottery jackpot. Just before going to bed on a Wednesday night when the moon is waxing, enter your room without turning on the light and, in the dark, pray to the guardian spirits of your home to help you improve your financial situation with a lottery win. Then approach each corner of your room and say:

> *Dea Fortuna, rosa mia, fammi vedere la sorte mia.*

> Goddess Fortuna, my rose, let me see my destiny.

When you go to sleep, you will receive messages in your dreams that you must not tell anyone, nor must you tell anyone of this spell. Record your dreams on paper as soon as you wake. Use *La Smorfia* (the dream dictionary that assigns numbers to words for the sole purpose of playing the lottery) to interpret your dreams/numbers, and you will win a substantial sum.

I know what you're thinking: "Where am I supposed to get a copy of *La Smorfia*?" I have included the traditional list in chapter 6. However, there are literally books dedicated to *La Smorfia*. For a more modern interpretation, search "La Smorfia Napolitana" on the Internet. It will require some work translating Neapolitan to Italian and then Italian to English, but it can be fun. Good luck!

Mother-in-Law

Suppose no matter how much you try, your mother-in-law simply doesn't like you. What is a girl (or boy) to do? There are many variations of this spell. Here are three.

First, you need to obtain some sugar or honey from your mother-in-law's kitchen. Find out what her favorite cookie or cake is. Then make it for her (and this is the challenging part) with the utmost love in your heart using the sugar/honey you liberated from her kitchen unbeknownst to her. When finished, invite your mother-in-law over for coffee and serve her favorite treat.

Second, you need to smuggle sugar from your kitchen into your mother-in-law's kitchen. Specifically, you must replace the sugar she uses to sweeten her coffee with the sugar from your kitchen. With repeated use of your sugar, your mother-in-law will sweeten toward you.

Lastly, your other option would be to do all the above plus serve her coffee where you have added one drop of blood from your ring finger (literally the finger you wear your engagement and/or wedding ring on). Make sure the coffee is black and screaming hot when you do and stir it (clockwise) well.

If your mother-in-law really hates you, or you have reason to believe she has cursed you, you may have to resort to serving her coffee that you have secretly spat in. This must be done on a Tuesday during a waning moon. When you greet her hello, you must kiss her three times. Her left, her right, and then her left cheek. This will rid you of the curse and return it right back to her. The same must be repeated when you leave. Be careful. If your mother-in-law has, in fact, cursed you, she will pick up on what you're doing and will refuse the coffee, which now is the least of your worries!

Assessing the Effect of Prayers and/or Spell Work via Dream Interpretation

Even before observing the material result of your spell work, you can assess whether it has taken effect through dream interpretation. Dreams give insight on the external forces influencing the situation.

Spell work typically follows a question/answer model. The prayer or spell work "asks," and the "answer" typically comes through dreams and visions prior to the result materializing in real life. Dreams can be experienced during sleep, or they can be daydreams.

The answer can be passive, as in something you, as a third party, see in your dream. Or the answer can be active, as in something you are doing in the dream.

Sometimes you receive a message indicating whether your spell worked. Other times you may receive a message regarding what action you need to take. These dream symbols may just be used to predict the outcome and/or interpret the influences surrounding you at the time of the dream. You will only know how it works for you by using it regularly. It is very important to keep a dream journal. You can then make notes beside your recorded dreams for future interpretation. How I work it is to record my dreams. I then make a note about the known symbolism and what I think it may mean. I then go back and make a note about its meaning based on the actual outcome.

Here is a list of things you may see in your dreams and their meaning. These are dreams where you are the observer and not the participant. You can then use these symbolic meanings to interpret the answer to your prayer or spell work.

To see a/an:

Abbott/Pope/High Priest: Proceed with caution.

Adulterer: Betrayal by a man.

Altar: Death.

Ants: Earnings.

Bees: Cannot continue like this/cannot live like this.

Bell (ringing): News.

Birds: It is out of your grasp; it will leave you; there's no point in pursuing it.

Blind person: It will come.

Blood: Joy.

Boat: Things are looking up. Troubles are passing.

Bread: Wealth.

Breasts: Pregnancy.

Cadaver(s): Bad omen.

Candles (burning): Death.

Car: Will flee/escape. Everything will happen quickly.

Cat: Running out of luck.

Child (female): Bad omen.

Child (male): Your luck will improve.

Children: Everything has come to a halt.

Cigarettes: Wealth.

Clock: In time, you will succeed.

Coercion: Sorrow.

Cooking: You will soon see the result you wanted.

Cow(s) (black): Joy.

Cow(s) (white): Respect.

Crow: Death.

Dancing: A party.

Death: Long life.

Defecating: Contempt.

Dog: Loyalty.

Donkey: With hard work, you will obtain your goal.

Doves: Lovers.

Eclipse: Bad omen.

Farmer: Expect good things.

Fire: Baptism (literal and figurative).

Fire (blazing): Passionate love.

Fish: Abundance.

Flames: People are speaking badly of you; gossip.

Flowers: Marriage.

Frog: Bad sign.

Garden (of flowers): Misfortune.

Ghost: The problem will fade away.

Goat: Abundance.

Goose: It's going to take a very long time.

Hen: All is lost.

High Priestess: You must resign yourself to the situation/outcome.

Horse (black): Bad outcome/omen.

Horse (white): Good outcome/omen.

Hotel: Honeymoon.

Hunchback (female): Bad sign.

Hunchback (male): Good luck.

Insects: Short illness or an inexperienced magician is attempting to harm the subject.

Kissing (friends): Excellent news.

Kissing (long-time enemies): All is lost.

Kissing (lovers): Loyalty.

Kissing (women): Betrayal.

Lake: All is done.

Lamb: They are innocent.

Lamp: There is love; love will be renewed.

Man (drunk): The man in question is a bad man.

Man (gentleman): You are in good company.

Man (old): A lot of time.

Man (young): Acceptance.

Money: Financial misfortune.

Moon: Good sign.

People: Entertainment.

Priest: Bad omen.

Rainbow: Someone will soon return.

River: Sorrow.

Rooster: Birth.

Roses (pink): Innocent love.

Roses (red): Lust, passion, romantic love.

Roses (white): Death or a woman.

Roses (yellow): Jealousy.

Scorpion: Danger.

Sea (angry waves): Bad sign; can't do anything about it.

Sea (calm): The love affair is over.

Sewing: You will be deceived.

Sewing needles: People are speaking ill of you. You are afflicted with malocchio.

Shadows: It is all going to vanish.

Ship: Your fortune/soulmate is in another land.

Sky (lit up): A new love.

Snakes: Serious health scare or the subject of the dream is afflicted by black magic.

Soldiers: You are under the protection of archangels.

Star (falling): Love relationship ending.

Stars (fixed in the sky): As certain as death.

Sun: Your wish will be granted.

Table: Thank you. (For example, the saint is thanking you for the offering.)

Thief: Someone stole your lover.

Tree (bearing fruit): Impending fortune/abundance.

Tree (cut down): Heartbreak.

Tree (dead): It's all over.

Tree (flowering): Good outcome; love will blossom.

Tree (growing): Everything will be okay.

Umbrella: Best to consult a priest.

Water: Tears.

Waves (ocean): Bad.

Window (opening): New (good) beginning.

Wine: Sorrow.

Wolves: Bad company will result in your undoing.

Woman: Bad news.

Woman (blonde): Someone has cursed or cast a spell on you.

Woman (lactating): Much time will pass.

Woman (pregnant): Everything will be sorted out soon.

Chapter 10

Rituals

We all have rituals. Rituals are things we do that make us feel safe and in control. Rituals ground us and help us center ourselves amid chaos. I have rituals that I have been performing daily my entire life, and I am not even consciously aware of them unless someone points them out to me. I perform rituals that ground me and reconnect me to my roots. These rituals help me maintain my connection to my ancestors and my culture.

In this chapter, I will share with you some of my rituals. I am not doing this because I think you have to practice the same rituals. My desire is to first help you become aware of your existing rituals. My second desire is to inspire you to practice them mindfully, making them part of your spiritual and magical practice.

Our home is our church, and our meal prep area and supper table are our altars. Cooking and housekeeping rituals are a spiritual practice. Mundane tasks done mindfully place us in a meditative state. This meditative state is where we work our magic.

Make things. Make food from scratch. Make crafts. Garden. Sew. Crochet. Crafting places you in a meditative state. Practicing a craft that your ancestors practiced opens a direct line to them. You can ask them to help you. I have personally experienced taking up a new hobby such as knitting, which I had never been taught. My late mother was extremely talented, so I asked her for help and, in a very short while, marveled at what I could create as a beginner. Also, these things you make are charged with your love, your connection to your ancestors, your power, your magic.

Food is not merely fuel. Food is medicine. Food is magic. Food brings people together. Food is at the center of family traditions. Food is legacy in the form of recipes handed down for generations. Food is how we connect to our cultural roots. Food is how we connect to our ancestors. Food is sacred.

Let me begin with a blinding glimpse of the obvious: Italian culture is food centric.

We have rituals surrounding all kinds of food preparation. Every meal preparation, no matter how simple or elaborate, is a ritual. All food receives reverential treatment. Nothing is discarded. Nothing is wasted. If a dish should not turn out the way we want it to, no matter how unpleasant it may taste, we never utter the words "That's disgusting." This is because food, all food, is *la grazia di Dio* (the grace of God).

Morning Coffee

One ritual that many of us share is our morning coffee. Every morning, the first thing I do is make my way to my kitchen. I grind the coffee beans, always an espresso roast, and then put the coffee on. The aroma of the coffee wakes my senses. While enjoying my first cup of coffee, I relax my mind and plan my day. On the rare occasion that I must rush out in the morning, I pack my coffee in a travel mug. Sure, I get my morning caffeine in, but I miss the centering ritual. On the weekend, when I am not as regimented, I may sleep in a couple hours or get caught up with other things. However, my day doesn't officially commence until I have made and enjoyed my first cup of coffee. When I travel, I take my coffee wherever I can get it. I don't feel the same centering I feel at home from going through my ritual of grinding the beans, selecting the coffeepot (I have a variety), and selecting my favorite mug. I carry out this ritual every morning, and during this process, my mind enters a meditative state. This state clears my mind for the day ahead.

Afternoon Coffee

In the middle of the afternoon when I'm feeling stressed or too inside my own head, I stop whatever I am doing and brew some coffee using my stovetop moka coffeemaker. As the coffee comes up to the top of the coffee maker, the aroma permeates my entire home. Afternoon coffee always centers me. Occasionally, I'll have a biscotti for added enjoyment. It soothes the child inside. Afternoon coffee always recalls all those afternoon coffees of my childhood. All the conversations. All the aunts and uncles that are long gone. All the stories they told. It relaxes and energizes me and just makes me feel centered. Sometimes I even feel one of my parents close to me.

Supper

Supper is the one meal of the day when we all sit down together as a family, no matter what. I realize this ritual is old-fashioned. I prepare supper every day. I was raised this way and wish to pass this tradition on to my children. The look on my family's face when they follow the aroma to the kitchen makes my heart happy. Some days it's a full meal cooked that day. Other times it is leftovers from the night before. Doesn't matter what it is; all that matters is that it is prepared with love and we spend time together. The ritual of preparing helps me sort out my thoughts and desires. I have lost count of how many wonderful situations I have manifested in my life. All these manifestations began as daydreams and wishes I entertained while preparing a meal. I would be preparing vegetables and absentmindedly think to myself, "Wouldn't it be wonderful if . . ." or "Oh, how I wish . . ." and within months, sometimes even as quickly as days, that something wonderful would become reality.

Sunday Dinner

The ritual of Sunday gravy or sauce is the most unifying. The smell of meatballs frying first thing on Sunday morning. The aroma of the meat slowly braising in tomato sauce permeates the home. I may live too far from my old friends and family, but when we do speak, we reconnect over "What did you cook on Sunday?" I often go weeks without making Sunday gravy. When I am feeling the need for some comfort or when I am missing my parents and aunts and uncles that are no longer living, the ritual of preparing Sunday gravy always makes my house feel like home.

Grocery Shopping: Bringing the Food Home

In a food-centric culture, grocery shopping is much more than just a chore. I thank my dad for teaching me that grocery shopping is about celebrating the abundance in our life. My dad immigrated first to Canada and then the United States in 1952. He never forgot what it was like to be hungry and to have nothing. He never forgot how grateful he was for what he had, even when he hardly had anything.

Being able to go to a supermarket and buy fresh fruit and vegetables, meat, cheese, pasta, olive oil, and some sweets never got old. He looked like a little boy on Christmas day every single time he unpacked and put away the groceries. There was a whole ritual surrounding grocery shopping. Before going out, the fridge, freezer, and pantry were tidied and cleaned. This allowed for a full inventory of what we already had in the house. The walk around the supermarket was an exploration. My dad (unlike me) never brought a list. He went into the supermarket with an open mind and the desire to be surprised. I grew up buying what was in season decades before it became what fashionable chefs proclaim on television.

The real ritual was when we came home. My dad would carefully unpack every bag with love. He would hold a package of freshly sliced cold cuts to his nose, breathe it in, and say, "Ahhhh, beautiful," and lovingly place it in the fridge. When all the groceries were put away, he would open the fridge and say, "Look at this abundance! We are blessed." He would repeat the same thing with the freezer and the pantry. When I was a poor student living on my own, I would do the exact same ritual with the little food I could afford. I believe that because of this, when I had nothing, I always had enough food. Now that I am doing much better than those early days, my grocery ritual is very much the ritual I learned from my dad. I always celebrate the abundance we have been blessed with, and we always have abundance to celebrate.

Cleaning and Blessing the Home: La bella 'mbriana and il Munaciello

Cleaning the home is not just about removing dust. Cleaning the home is about clearing the energy in the home. Cleaning the home is about taking care of not just where you and your family live; it is an act of devotion to your home and the spirits that inhabit it.

I grew up where all homes had a hearth, and the hearth was used daily except during the summer months. Hearths were well maintained and always clean. My Neapolitan family referred to the spirit of the home and heart as *la bella 'mbriana* (the beautiful *'mbriana*).

The beautiful 'mbriana, for the people of Naples, is the name of the angel of the hearth and the bearer of fortunate events. She is a mysterious creature, a kind and benevolent presence, that brings wellness and health. La bella 'mbriana dwells permanently in a house placed under her protection.

When the beautiful 'mbriana does appear, her appearance is fleeting—perceived in our peripheral vision. She only appears for a few moments, perhaps by a curtain waving in the breeze of an open window or in the reflection of a window or in a dark corner of the house.

She appears as a very beautiful young woman, with a sweet face, a fairy. Legend has it that when we perceive the beautiful 'mbriana and attempt to look straight at her, she transforms into a butterfly or a gecko. Due to the connection with this whimsical fairy, the Neapolitans consider the gecko to be a lucky charm and are careful not to drive it away or disturb it.

It is customary to greet la bella 'mbriana when we come home. We typically say, "Hello, house," and when we leave, we charge our dog to "guard the house," and it is implied that "the house" (beautiful 'mbriana) is watching over all.

The old ones used to set a place at the table at every meal for the beautiful 'mbriana for fear she would be offended by their lack of hospitality and thus leave them and misfortune would befall the home. My family just kept an extra seat in the dining room and near the kitchen table for her. To this day, I keep an extra seat near my table, just in case.

You can feel her presence in the stillness and serenity of your home. That intangible, cozy, welcoming feeling.

The other spirit that inhabits our homes is 'O Munaciello (the little monk). This spirit is the most famous and feared by the Neapolitans. 'O Munaciello is a mischievous sprite, a trickster. This is the energy felt in a home when it is all closed up, and the air feels heavy and stale. This spirit feeds on discord. 'O Munaciello misplaces or breaks objects we need or care about and in turn will leave mysterious cash "tributes." You will find coins and money you didn't know you had in your pockets. If you do, you know he was there.

'O Munaciello loves misplacing things and watching us panic looking for them. He loves walking right behind us down dark hallways to freak us out. That uneasy feeling you get when you walk into a dark room, that's him. A messy home makes la bella 'mbriana retreat and 'O Munaciello play. 'O Munaciello is also the little jerk that invites malocchio into the home. He's like the anti-ward against malocchio. Have you ever had a day where everyone in the home is out of sorts? Everyone feels tired or on edge? Everyone feels like they are in a fog? That is 'O Munaciello running rampant in your home. You can subdue him with three malocchio removals aimed at the home and your family (do not forget to include your pets). This will buy you enough time to do a house blessing. But before you bless your home, I strongly recommend you tidy and clean your house first to wake up la bella 'mbriana. She keeps 'O Munaciello at bay.

When la bella 'mbriana is fully present, 'O Munaciello is hardly detected in the home. Keeping our home clean and uncluttered maintains this balance.

We are far busier than our ancestors were. Here is what you can do daily to keep your home spirits appeased and your home in balance. This is just a baseline. I tell you from experience that you will have best results doing both daily maintenance and a weekly full cleaning and blessing. Writing this book has resulted in me neglecting my home. I get the baseline done, mostly. However, I have not done the full weekly cleaning and blessing consistently, and I have experienced firsthand 'O Munaciello busting my chops. Things breaking down and going missing and then ten, and twenty-dollar bills appearing. I know what you're thinking. This doesn't sound too bad. Well, let me explain. The ten- and twenty-dollar bills are not even a drop in the bucket to replace the things that mysteriously broke down

La bella 'mbriana loves a clean and tidy home; light, beautiful aromas, such as fresh-brewed coffee; and home-cooked food and sweets.

My zia would always call out "Scètate bella 'mbriana!" ("Wake up, beautiful 'mbriana!") in the morning when she opened the windows. Whenever the energy in the home felt oppressive, she would toss salt on the floor and sweep it out the door, saying, "Vai via brutta bestia" ("Go away, ugly beast," referring to evil spirits).

Daily: At the Very Minimum

Make your bed and open your bedroom window to air it out.

Wash dishes.

Keep the table clean and clear between meals.

Remove clutter by entrances.

Weekly

Saturday is historically the Italian "clean and bless the house" day; however, for years, I worked a rotating schedule and so I did this on my first day off, whether it was Saturday or not.

Open all the windows to let the stale air out and the fresh air and sunlight in (when it is very cold out, I just leave them open five minutes).

Pick up clutter.

Do laundry.

Change and make the bed.

Wash dishes and tidy the kitchen, fridge, and pantry (in preparation for grocery shopping).

Clean the bathroom.

Dust furniture.

Sweep (sprinkle some salt on the floor and sweep it up). Collect the dust, dirt, and salt in a dustpan and toss it outside.

Mop floors (with a splash of vinegar and some salt added to the water).

Dust and vacuum (I sprinkle a little salt on the rug before vacuuming).

When I am done, I light a brand-new candle or some sweet-smelling incense.

La bella 'mbriana's serene and loving presence is almost tangible. I almost forgot: la bella 'mbriana also grants wishes. She grants wishes confided to her when you are cleaning house or preparing food.

Some of her favorite foods are homemade: ciambella (donut-shaped cake), bread, and pizza. She also loves the aroma of fresh coffee and cinnamon.

There are other spirits residing in and around our homes. I will discuss them in chapter 13.

When Something Breaks
or No Longer Works

When an object breaks or stops working, it must be given proper treatment. First, everything must be done to try to repair it. If it cannot be repaired, thank it for its service and discard it appropriately; never just shove it in a corner of your house. Following the ritual of thanking the object for its service releases the spirit in the object, freeing it to inhabit the new replacement. I like to think of it as object reincarnation.

When We No Longer Need Something

Sometimes we come to the conclusion that we no longer need an object, but it is still fully functional. First, try to rehome it to friends and family. If someone does need it, thank it for its service and inform it of its new home. It must be cleaned before giving it away so that it can be released of the energy of your home. If no one you know wants it, still thank it and release it, and after cleaning it, donate it to charity.

When We Bring New Items Home

Whenever we bring something new into our home, it must be washed or cleaned before we use it. Cleaning or washing it removes the various energetic imprints left by other people. Imagine how many people have touched this item—from the raw materials used to make it to the people handling it in the store. Welcome it into the home the same way you welcome someone coming to live with you. Treating objects this way enhances their performance and they last longer. There is a spirit living in every object in your home. Always welcome it when it arrives and thank it when it is time for it to leave you.

Why Rituals Work

Rituals create boundaries and make us feel safe. Rituals set the stage for an expected outcome. Rituals return us to center and ground us. Rituals renew our connection with the spirit world and our ancestors. This interaction brings peace, love, and magic into our homes.

Ritual is as simple as making things. Make food. Create art. Learn to sew, crochet, knit, paint, sculpt, etc. Make as many things as you can rather than buying them. Because everything you make is magic.

Chapter 11

Malocchio (The Evil Eye)

Malocchio is a popular belief that a look or glance from one person can send misfortune and bodily symptoms to the person being looked at. The most characteristic element of the evil eye, as its name implies, is that it is cast with a look. It is believed that when one looks upon another with envy, they can inflict that which they look upon with a mild state of spiritual illness. Belief in malocchio is not limited to Italians. Almost every culture in the world has their version of the malocchio.

I have come across two opposing views on how malocchio is transmitted. The more widely shared belief is that it is unintentional. However, there are people, and I have met them, who have the ability to inflict malocchio intentionally. The caster uses their eyes to channel negative energy toward a specific person: an intense look often accompanied by flattery or insults or mean wishes is often the hallmark of this phenomenon.

Causes and types of malocchio are varied but all along the same lines. Malocchio can be sent because of strong feelings such as anger, envy, jealousy, possessive love, passion, and obsession. Often those who afflict others with the evil eye are not fully aware of it. It can be as simple as someone has angered you and you look at them from across the room and think to yourself, "Damn them!" or "I hope something bad happens to them!" Another example is a friend who is wearing her brand-new boots. You look at them and say, "I love your boots; they are so nice!" but in your mind, you are thinking, full of envy, "I love those boots; I want them." Later that same day, your friend might step in something, ruining her new boots, or, worse, injure herself while wearing them.

Symptoms caused by malocchio are typically mild to moderate when compared to a fattura (spell) or maledizione (curse). A mild case may cause a sudden streak of bad luck. Unusual clumsiness. Objects seeming to fly out of your hands and crash onto the floor. Objects breaking in your hands without the use of any force. Among the most common moderate symptoms are headache, specifically behind the eyes. Some people experience swelling of one or both eyes. Drowsiness. Fatigue. A feeling of despair. A feeling of impending doom without reason. Low mood without cause. Loss of focus or concentration. Obsessive thoughts on a specific thing. You may also feel anxious and fearful without apparent reason.

If the malocchio is sent because of strong feelings of love and obsession, the afflicted person's symptoms will also include sudden unexplainable thoughts of attraction or obsession towards the caster. Sudden disagreements and quarrels with their current partner. Feeling like there is a wall between them and their current partner. Intrusive thoughts about the caster, often just before going to sleep. The afflicted person will dream of the caster. These dreams will not be pleasant nor obvious. These dreams will be puzzling or disturbing. One example of a puzzling dream is that the caster will appear in the afflicted person's dreams, but either will not speak to them or will ignore them completely. Another example is the caster will appear in dreams and the dreamer will want them sexually, but the caster in the dream behaves as if they do not notice. There are many variations of these symptoms and dreams, but they are all quickly recognized by an experienced healer.

How to Diagnose Malocchio
Using Water and Oil

Typically, the method to diagnose and cure malocchio is taught by a mature healer to a young successor on Christmas Eve. This is how I learned. However, over the many years I have been practicing, I have not seen any evidence that learning it any other way makes it any less effective.

There are as many methods as there are healers. Some read the configuration of the oil on water literally. For example, if the drops of oil behave one way, the test is positive for malocchio; if they behave another way, the test is negative for malocchio. Then there are the healers who read the oil by interpreting the way the oil moves around on the water and the shapes and patterns it creates to determine whether the person is afflicted. The following is, in my experience, the most common procedure.

What You Will Need

A shallow, white porcelain bowl

A small pitcher of water

A bottle of oil

A teaspoon

Salt

Scissors

Fill the bowl halfway with water from the small pitcher. Using a teaspoon, drop three to five drops of oil into the water. Carefully, without moving the contents of the bowl, place the bowl on the head of the person you are diagnosing. Observe the oil.

If the oil drops migrate toward each other and merge, malocchio is present.

If the oil drops burst and spread out over the surface of the water "appearing" to disappear, malocchio is present.

If the oil drops do not change at all, malocchio is not present.

How to Cure Malocchio

If malocchio is present, recite the following charm (some leave the bowl on the person's head while they do this; other people place the bowl on the table). This *scongiuro* (or charm) is a traditional one used by my family from the Abruzzo region. For years, I have been promoting the recitation of charms in the original language. You don't have to know the language. Read it phonetically. There is magic in these words that have been handed down for generations.

We always begin a malocchio cure by calling Saint Michael:

The shield of Saint Michael Archangel is above me,

The shield of Saint Michael Archangel is below me,

The shield of Saint Michael Archangel is beside me,

The sword of Saint Michael Archangel is before me,

The shield of Saint Michael Archangel is behind me,

The fire of Saint Michael Archangel surrounds and defends me,

Amen.

Then we begin the malocchio cure charm:

San Sisto, San Sisto,

lo spirito tristo,

e mala morte,

di giorno e di notte,

tu caccia da questa,

tu caccia da noi,

tu strappa e calpesta,

ogni occhio che nuoce,

qui faccio la croce.

Saint Sisto, Saint Sisto,

throughout the day and throughout the night,

drive away from this person,

drive away from us,

this dark spirit,

and miserable death,

tear out, stomp on,

every eye that seeks to harm,

Here I do the sign of the cross.

With open scissors, use one point to make the sign of the cross three times to "cut up" the merged oil (in the case of merged oil) or the smeared oil.

Then hold the scissors with both hands and cut the air above the bowl three times. Put aside the scissors and add three pinches of salt to the bowl, reciting the following:

Lunedi Santo, Martedi Santo, Mercoledi Santo, Giovedi Santo, Venerdi

Santo, Sabato Santo, e Domenica di Pasqua,

In nome di Criste, crepa l'occhio triste!

Holy Monday, Holy Tuesday, Holy Wednesday, Holy Thursday,
    Holy Friday,

Holy Saturday, and Easter Sunday,

In the name of Christ, the evil eye bursts!

Dip your right thumb in the bowl and, using your right thumb, trace the sign of the cross:

» three times on the person's forehead between the eyes

» three times on the back of their neck

» three times over their heart

Pour the contents of the bowl onto the ground or down the drain.

As the healer, you then take a moment to yourself to thank Saint Michael for his protection and pray:

San Michele Arcangelo,

difendici nella battaglia contro le insidie e la malvagità del demonio,

sii nostro aiuto.

Te lo chiediamo supplici che il Signore lo comandi.

E tu, principe della milizia celeste,

con la potenza che ti viene da Dio,

ricaccia nell'inferno Satana e gli altri spiriti maligni,

che si aggirano per il mondo a perdizione delle anime.

Amen.

Saint Michael, the Archangel,

defend us in battle.

Be our protection against the wickedness and snares of the devil.

May God rebuke him, we humbly pray;

and do Thou, O Prince of the Heavenly Host,

by the Divine Power of God,

cast into hell Satan and all the evil spirits

who roam throughout the world seeking the ruin of souls.

Amen.

How to Ward Against Malocchio

Sleep with an open scissors under your bed with the points at your feet and the handles at your head.

Wear an amulet. There are so many to choose from (see list in chapter 7).

If you find you are very susceptible to the evil eye, you may have better results wearing an amulet containing carnelian or coral.

Don't brag or flaunt.

When someone compliments you, thank them and then find some privacy and spit on the ground three times.

Share your good news only with people who love you.

Take a purifying bath once per week. To turn a regular bath into a purifying bath, add a cup of salt to the bathwater.

Pray to Saint Michael Archangel.

Pray the Rosary.

Chapter 12

Curses

A curse, hex, or jinx is a malediction that is intentionally perpetrated on the victim. The malefactor targets an individual and carries out a ritual with the purpose of harming someone with magic. Symptoms are moderate to severe and can be quite frightening. This type of spell is tenacious, because it is fueled by hate, jealousy, and depravity, and it feeds on the fear of the target. To remove a curse, the practitioner must know how to curse. It does not require special skills or expensive items to put a curse on someone. All it requires is motivation and intent to do harm. Contrary to what charlatans and con artists want you to believe, it does not require thousands of dollars and "special candles from Jerusalem" to remove a curse. It requires a highly skilled and experienced practitioner well versed in both malediction and benediction. One must know how to curse in order to know how to reverse it.

As explained in the preceding chapter, malocchio, or the evil eye, is the belief that if someone looks or gazes at you with the slightest bit of envy in their hearts (knowingly or unknowingly), their gaze can afflict you with negative energy that can wreak havoc in your body and your life. Symptoms of malocchio can be mild (a headache, visual disturbances, indigestion, an unsettled feeling, clumsiness). Whereas symptoms of a curse can be moderate to severe (a migraine, nausea and vomiting, extreme anxiety, accidents resulting in broken bones, burns, or any other physical injury), unexplained financial or relationship problems—think common cold versus influenza viruses. The most susceptible are people already in a weakened state either physically or emotionally, the very young, and the very old. It is believed malocchio can cause severe symptoms and even death in the frail, the very young and the very old.

The difference between a curse and malocchio is, with a curse, someone has intentionally infected you and you will most likely need to have it removed by magic (antibiotic). Malocchio is akin to a virus. You are susceptible to catching it when you are feeling emotionally and spiritually run down. You can *prevent* catching it by taking care of yourself mentally, emotionally, and spiritually. You can also *rid* yourself of malocchio by taking care of yourself mentally, emotionally, and spiritually. A curse is akin to an infection and it requires taking action with magic (antibiotic).

Binding/Freezing Spells

Whenever the conversation turns to curses, binding, or protection spells, I am always reminded of my great aunt Zia Paolina. My Zia Paolina was my paternal grandmother's little sister and a widow. She was born in 1906 and, in 1920, at the age of fourteen, left her home town in Abruzzo to find adventure in Naples. It was outrageous at that time for an unmarried girl to be out on her own, and compared to her village in Abruzzo, Naples was a wild and exciting city. Zia Paolina spent half her life in Naples and Sicily. She spoke many dialects of Italian, as well as French and English fluently. Unmarried and financially independent, she emigrated to the United States in the 1950s. In America, she met up with a third cousin from her hometown in Abruzzo. He was a widower with grown children. They married and were together until he passed away roughly ten years later. I remember my Zia Paolina as a strong, independent, fearless, cunning, and powerful woman. She was a feminist with looks and wit reminiscent of Maude, the character played by Bea Arthur in the TV program of the same name from the 1970s.

Every summer we would drive down to Massachusetts, to visit her. Zia Paolina was the closest thing I had to a grandmother nearby, since her sister, my nonna, lived in Italy. Her house was full of interesting stuff, and her small kitchen had two fridges. One hot and muggy July afternoon, my Zia Paolina said to me: "Mary-Grace, go in the icebox and get us some ice cream." I got up from my chair and walked toward the closest fridge. Just as my hand landed on the door handle, my great-aunt slammed her hand on the table and shouted, "NO, NOT THAT ONE! I keep my enemies in there. The other icebox." My dad quickly looked at his aunt and, in our dialect, asked: "Who exactly do you keep in there?" Zia Paolina winked at me and replied to her nephew: "Don't worry. They all deserved it." We stayed the night. I slept on a cot in the kitchen. No, that's not true. I couldn't sleep, because all I could think about was Zia Paolina's enemies in the icebox. I remember thinking they were literally shrunken down and crammed into that tiny icebox. I was six years old. It freaked me right out. As I got older, I envisioned her enemies dismembered and packed in the freezer.

The summer I turned fourteen was the last time we would visit Zia Paolina in her own home. She was going blind from diabetes, and she wasn't coping very well on her own. She and I were sitting on the porch this hot, muggy, July afternoon, and she took my hand and said, "I'm old. I'm blind. Yesterday I shit myself. I think it's time." She got up from her chair and led me into her kitchen. She opened "the other icebox" and revealed its contents to me. It wasn't packed with shrunken bodies or frozen body parts. It was packed with . . . little packages wrapped in tinfoil with black string tied around them. "I'll show you how, but first I gotta get something." She went into her bedroom for a few minutes. When she came out, she had a ragged little prayer book, a really beat-up deck of Italian playing cards, and a few really worn saint prayer cards. She then tied a red ribbon to my left wrist, mumbled something I couldn't make out, and kissed me on the top of my head. Then she stood up and said, "Now let me show you how to protect yourself from people who mean you harm."

How to Freeze (or Bind) Your Enemy from Doing Magic against You

<u>What You Will Need</u>

A photograph of your enemy (make sure it is only of the person you wish to bind)

Small sewing scissors

Sewing needle

Black thread

Black ribbon or yarn

Begin by cutting the eyes and hands of your enemy (if their hands are in the photo) out of the photograph and burn them. (Zia Paolina used her lit cigarette.)

Then thread the needle with black thread and sew the mouth in the photo shut.

<u>Incantation:</u>

We cut out the eyes, so they can't look (malocchio).

We cut off the hands, so they can't gesture (curse).

We sew up the mouth, so they can't speak (incantations).

We tie them up, so they are bound from doing us harm.

Then fold the photo up tightly, wrap it in tinfoil, and tie a black ribbon/string around it. Place the little package at the back of the freezer to be kept there until you decide it is safe to release them.

Control/Obsession

To Make Someone Fall Madly and Obsessively in Love with You

This is classic moon magic of Neapolitan origin. This spell is done on the night of the new moon. The woman (or man) who wants someone to fall madly in love with them will entrust their desire in the power of the new moon.

Buonanotte luna nuova,

Buonanotte luna nuova,

Sei venuta e che m'hai portato?

Braccia di cera e cosce di piombo.

Good night new moon,

Good night new moon,

You have come and what have you brought me?

Arms of wax and legs of lead.

Make a doll representing that person with arms of wax and legs of lead. Then wrap this doll in a white cloth and tie it up using nine knots to irreversibly bind the object of your desire to you. Once the doll is prepared, recite the following invocation to the moon over the wrapped doll as each knot is tied.

Legami (the name of the person),

Tu me lo devi legar nelle braccia, nel pensiero e nella volontà.

Tranne che me tutto possa scordar.

Quando questo nodo si andrà a snodar.

Bind to me (the name of the person),

You must bind their arms, their thoughts, and their will to me.

May they forget and forsake all else, except for me.

Until this knot unknots itself.

The following is most likely why we were taught to never accept food or drink when we visit people's homes—unless our parents say it is okay! More *fatture d'amore* (love spells):

1. In a small pot, preferably made of copper, add some water, some drops of blood taken from your ring finger, and a hair belonging to the object of your desire. Bring the water to a boil. Once the water has boiled, remove the hair and add a small amount of the water to a glass of wine and offer it to the the object of your desire to drink so that they will instantly fall in love with you.

2. Bake a cake after adding some drops of blood from your ring finger to the batter. Once the cake is cooled, feed it only to the man/woman you want to fall in love with you.

3. Add a few drops of menstrual blood (or if you are a man, semen) to coffee and offer it unknowingly to the man/woman you want to fall in love with you.

4. To make someone completely obsessed with you, offer them a glass of wine you prepared the night before. In a small jar, place some red wine, some drops of your menstrual blood (or semen), and some of your pubic hair. Shake it vigorously and place the jar under your bed when you will be expecting your lover. After you and your lover are done having intercourse, without being seen, take the small jar somewhere that you can strain the contents into another clean container. Add a few drops of this elixir to a glass of wine or coffee and offer it to your lover. They will quickly become obsessed with you.

I want to share one instance that ended tragically. A lady was referred to me for a magical consultation and reading because she had cast this spell on her brother-in-law (her sister's husband). She told me how although she too, like him, was married with children, she had always been in love with him and couldn't live without him. She carried out her spell and was thrilled and amazed at how quickly it worked! Within a couple of days, they were seeing each other secretly and thus began their torrid affair. After having intercourse with him *one* time, she tired of him. She described to me how she suddenly lost interest. She told him it was a one-time thing, a mistake, and that it was over.

This man was known to be a practical, pragmatic, stable man. A good husband and father. A pillar of the community. But after she told it him it was over, something in him snapped, and he became a completely different person. He became obsessed with her. He stopped going to work and neglected his obligations, including his family. He phoned her all day long begging and pleading and proclaiming his love to her. He told his wife (her sister) that he was sorry, but his love for her sister was "bigger than him and out of his control." Her previously kindhearted, loving, devoted husband had been replaced by a complete stranger. His wife was devastated. She had a nervous breakdown and was hospitalized. Her school-aged children were left with their father, who, in his obsessive state, neglected them, so they fended for themselves, wanting no help from their aunt (the spellcaster).

The woman's husband threw her out. Her children (teenagers) refused to see or speak to her. Her entire family turned against her, and her brother-in-law became only more obsessed with her every day.

Three months to the day that she cast the spell, her brother-in-law was found by his children. While his wife was at work and his children in school, he hanged himself. All he left was a love letter to his sister-in-law pinned to his shirt stating: "If I cannot be with you, I have no reason to live."

Revenge

Lemon Curse

This revenge curse is done on Christmas Eve. A lemon is taken to midnight mass. At the part of the mass when the priest raises the chalice, you should discreetly nibble (or pick off with your fingernails) bits of lemon rind. When you return home, stick each "bite" with pins ,saying, "Tanti spinguli, tanti malanni" ("Many pins, many illnesses"). To curse your target, you then need to hide this stuck lemon somewhere in their home or toss it onto the roof of their house without being seen. If you fail to do this, you can leave the fruit with all the pins stuck anywhere on the victim's property for a whole night.

You can use a rag doll instead of a lemon, if you prefer. In this case, during the mass, the doll—hidden, of course—must be abused by twisting and pinching it, subsequently skewering it with pins when you get home, and hidden in the same manner as described above.

If you were to find these fruits or puppets of *Magaria* (witchcraft) in your home or on your property, all you would need to do to undo the curse is remove the pins and burn the lemon or doll. The malefic effects of the curse will cease immediately.

Removal

To Rid Your Home of a Curse
(Consists of Two Steps: Banishing and Blessing)

To break a curse and drive out the evil spirits from your home, first send your family out of the house. Once you are alone, unbraid or undo your hair if it is long and bare your breasts. Walk around your home with a pail of salted water and, with your dominant hand, take some water and throw (or sprinkle) it on every wall and floor of every room of the house. In a commanding voice, say,

Acqua e sali mè Signuri, pi livari la fattura,

acqua e sali San Giuvanni, p'astutari stu focu granni,

acqua e sali pi li magari, và fattura e nun turnari!

Water and salt, my Lord, to remove this curse,

Water and salt, Saint John, to put out this big fire,

Water and salt for the witches, go away, curse, and never return!

To bless your home and ward it against evil spirits, take some salt and toss it on every floor in your home. Sweep your home and sweep the salt out your entrance door. Now open all your windows and light up some church incense (or whichever incense you like to use for purification). While the incense burns, toss a pinch of salt in every corner of every room.

Remember to cover your breasts when you're done!

Chapter 13

Working with Spirits

Spirits are all around us. Whether we believe in them or not, they are present. Becoming acquainted and developing relationships with them is as simple, if not more so, as becoming acquainted with people. As with people, maintaining these relationships does require work. I refer to all spirits who guide, help, and work with us as spirit guides.

My earliest memories involve spirits. Angels, more recently deceased relatives, ancestors, saints, fairies—they are all very real and members of our extended family. Communing with them is in our customs and in our language. We don't sit or stand on the dinner table because angels live there. Our deceased parents and grandparents are not forgotten once we are done grieving. Oh, no. Once we are done grieving their loss, we transition to our new relationship with them as spirits who are just as present in our daily lives, if not more so.

Guardian Angel

One of my earliest memories as a very small child was being taught to pray to my guardian angel. It has been forty-five years, yet I still remember the prayer the sisters (Franciscan nuns) taught us in nursery school. The day did not begin until we recited it:

Angelo di Dio, che sei il mio custode, illuminami, custodiscimi, reggi e governa me che ti fui affidato dalla pietà celeste. Amen.

Angel of God, my guardian dear, to whom His love entrusts me here, ever this day be at my side to light and guard, to rule and guide. Amen.

Our guardian angel is with us always. From the moment we are born and up until we take our last breath, they are there. This spirit guide's job is to watch over us but not interact or interfere. However, in extreme cases, especially involving our personal safety, they are permitted to act.

An example of this would be if you ever had the experience of absentmindedly stepping into traffic and felt as though someone grabbed you and pulled you back, only to turn around and find no one was there. That was your guardian angel.

If you've ever had the sensation that someone was standing right behind you, that was your guardian angel. You can also feel your guardian angel as a very light pressure on your head. It feels like a hand gently and just barely touching the surface of your hair. Take notice the next time you feel this sensation. Record what was going on and how you were feeling. I personally notice this sensation when I need reassurance or when I am on the right track.

You also may have heard your guardian angel. First thing in the morning, maybe you forgot to set your alarm. You abruptly wake up from a voice calling your name right beside your ear. You are certain you heard a voice. You look around, but no one is there. You ask your family, but no one else has heard a thing. These spirit guides appear as "imaginary" friends to children who need them. I place imaginary in quotation marks because they are not imaginary.

Your guardian angel can also materialize into a human or animal form. When this occurs, you will not be aware that that person or animal was your guardian angel. It is a realization that occurs after the fact. Our guardian angel is there to guide and to guard us. They can serve as messenger to a third party. If you've ever gone to see a psychic or if you yourself are a psychic, the messages received by the psychic are most often obtained from the seeker's (the person obtaining the reading) guardian angel. Typically, we do not involve our guardian angel in magic spells, but for one exception. In spells designed to mend a relationship, for instance, some practitioners may ask their guardian angel to speak on their behalf to the guardian angel of the person they wish to mend the relationship with.

To develop a relationship with your guardian angel, acknowledge their presence. Talk to them. If you are happy, tell them. If you are sad, tell them. If you are worried—especially if you are worried—take some time to unburden yourself with them. Seriously, they are here for you and you alone. Reach out to them. When things are going well, make it a point of sharing your happiness with your guardian angel. It is also good for you to hear yourself saying out loud when things are going well. Do something fun and invite them to come along. Or just simply remember to thank them for always being there. The more you interact with your guardian angel, the more they will make their presence felt.

Ask your angel for gifts. Don't be specific; just simply ask them for gifts. Then pay attention to what comes your way. The gift can be as simple as finding the last empty seat in a crowded bus. It can also be amazing. Years ago, I left my document folder on a train. I realized it too late. I was already outside the station and the train was long gone. Incredibly stressed, I was beside myself because I was visiting a different country, and my folder contained my passport and other valuable documents. I hailed a taxi. I got in the taxi and choked back tears all the way to my destination. When we arrived, I paid and got out of the taxi. Just as I began to walk away, the taxi driver called me by my name (I had not told him my name and I had paid cash) and said, "You forgot something." It was my document folder.

Other Angels

Your guardian angel is with you always. Other angels come in and out of your life depending on what you are experiencing. These other angels will work unseen; they may even materialize into human or animal form. Angels also work through other human beings.

We treat the surface where food is prepared and where food is eaten as sacred because angels live there. When I was a young girl, I spent a few summers in my father's hometown in Abruzzo. These summers were spent learning what "all good wives need to know how to do." I spent my summer vacation learning to do laundry by hand (believe it or not, there is an art to it), sewing, embroidering, cooking, and crocheting. A girl cousin about the same age as me and I went to the convent every day where we learned these crafts. This is where I learned that angels who specialize in specific skills can be called on to help us.

Suor Matilde (Sister Matilda), a nun who taught my dad when he was in nursery school (too cool not to mention), took me aside one day because I was extremely frustrated with my embroidery project. She patiently showed me each stitch and then dropped her voice to a whisper and said, "Ask the embroidery angels to help you. As a matter of fact, whenever you practice any skill, ask the angel of that skill to help you. You will learn faster and do it better than anyone else." Then she put her index finger to her lips for me to not tell anyone what she just said.

It's been over forty years, and to this day, whenever I am learning a new skill or practicing an old one, I always call on the angel of that skill. I always obtain better results when I do. I've even called on specializing angels to assist people who were assisting me. Whenever I or a member of my family has had a medical emergency, I always call on the medical angel to be present to make sure everything goes well. I really believe this to be the reason we have received nothing short of excellent care—even when under the care of a professional I have witnessed to be less than caring or competent. It was because an angel was truly watching over us.

Angels love to help us. They want us to call upon them to do stuff for us. I can prove it to you. Here is an experiment for you to carry out on your own: ask them for mundane things that make your life easier. Once you witness how consistent they are, you will feel confident asking them to help you with more involved things.

Because I believe there are angels who specialize, I have experiences that confirm that belief. Here are some mundane things I always ask for and they never disappoint:

Parking spaces: I ask the angels to find me the best parking space wherever I go, especially when I go somewhere I know parking is a real challenge. I am not specific about the location of the space, only that it must be the best space available. When I arrive at my destination and carefully look for a parking space, I am always blown away by what I find. This never gets old.

Personal shoppers: Seriously, this too never ceases to amaze me. My dad insisted they exist, and his and my own experiences have taught me that there are angels who specialize in leading us to specific items we ask for and those things are on sale. Now that my dad is on the other side, it could be him! I will think the following out loud: "I need to buy _____." This can be groceries, clothing, a book, nonessentials like cosmetics, anything really. Within a couple of days, the thought will pop in my head to go to a specific store (or website). There, I will find exactly what I said I needed . . . on sale. No fail. How many times have I said to my husband how unbelievable it was that when I do our grocery shopping, almost everything on my list is on sale! I don't even need to leaf through store flyers. I just go to whatever store (at times the same stores; other times, I get the idea to go to a completely different one) pops in my head, and there it all is . . . on sale. This, too, never gets old.

Try it out. Try it out with your angels and document your results. You can try out my examples or something that makes your life easier. If you are a salesperson, ask your angels to lead you to people looking to buy. Just try it; you have nothing to lose and so much to gain.

Ancestors

The word *ancestor* suggests faceless antecedents who lived hundreds of years ago. That said, I also honor my antecedents who lived hundreds of years ago, but not in the same way. When I speak of honoring and working with my ancestors, I mean my most immediate relatives who are deceased—my parents, aunts, uncles, grandparents, great-grandparents, great-great-grandparents. It is the constant retelling of their stories that keeps the line open, so to speak. Every time I retell their stories, I gain a deeper understanding of who I am. My children, who regrettably will never get to meet them, gain a little more understanding of where they came from and how it makes them who they are.

Examples of Working with Ancestors

Our ancestors knew how to make things. My dad and uncles knew how to make and fix things. I call upon them when I am making or fixing something. When I need to hire a contractor to do work, I call on them to supervise and make sure the contractor does the work I requested correctly. How do I know for sure my dad and uncles are present? If I am doing the work, I suddenly know how and obtain the exact result I wanted. Even if I've never done it before. How do I know my dad and uncles are present when a contractor comes to do a job at my home? I observe them with eyes that can tell if they are doing it right—even if I have never seen it in my life—and I hear myself asking very specific questions. It is absolutely amazing and, to be honest, it never gets old.

I am a homemaker at heart. I love cooking. I love crafting. I love creating. Food is central to Italian culture, and traditional recipes are the golden threads that link us to our ancestors.

Invite your ancestors to cook with you, if you haven't already. Even the most inexperienced cook will obtain an outstanding result by asking their ancestors to help. My ancestors have helped me find obscure, long-lost recipes. I have been able to replicate a late zia's signature dish so accurately that there is no doubt in my mind she cooked it through me. Something as common as tuna fish salad sand-wiches turns into a visit with my mom. When I want a tuna fish salad sandwich, not just any sandwich will do. This type of sandwich ranks number one on my list of comfort foods. Therefore, when I crave this sandwich, I want the tuna fish salad sandwich I remember from when I was little. My mom gave me her recipe ages ago, but mine never ended up tasting like I remember hers tasting. Since my mom passed away, I ask her to join me when I make it. I now re-create the exact salad my mom made when I was three years old. When I sit down to eat it, I always thank her, tell her I love her, and spend some time thinking about her. In those quiet moments, a memory I've long forgotten will pop in my head. Sometimes, I feel her stroke my hair.

Invite your ancestors in. You will be amazed how much you will learn about them and yourself. Research where they came from. Read history books. If you didn't have anyone to hand down their recipes to you, ask them to send them to you now. You will suddenly come across books, websites, etc. I know one man who found a long-lost recipe from his ancestors at a potluck. He and I would talk for hours about working with our ancestors. The conversation always turned to his longing for the dish his nonna made on Christmas day. He was too young at the time and couldn't figure it out. One day, his job held a potluck lunch before they closed for Christmas. He walked into the dining area to find a tray that looked and smelled exactly like his memories of his nonna's dish. He quickly searched for the coworker who brought it in. When he did, his coworker laughed and said, "I almost forgot about the potluck. I just threw that together from what was in my fridge. I'm glad you like it." My friend asked his coworker to describe what they used and how they prepared it. His nonna heard his longing and worked through his unsuspecting coworker. Now that's a Christmas miracle.

I love vintage perfume and have amassed a little collection over the years. I have three categories. Everyday, special occasions, and my favorite category, the perfumes worn by the people I love who have crossed over. No sense is tied as strongly to memory as our sense of smell. If I want to connect with my zia who raised me, opening my tiny bottle of Coty Emeraude perfume is all it takes to transport me forty years into the past. It feels as though I am standing right beside her. I instantly feel comforted. A few hours, maybe a couple of days later, I will see something or find something that she liked or she would always give me. That is her letting me know she is indeed nearby.

When working a healing or magic spell, I call upon my paternal grandmother and great-aunt. I call upon them because I know that they did this kind of work. When I do, I see the difference in the better results I obtain.

Honor your ancestors and feel their love course through your veins. Have a picnic at the cemetery where they are buried. Pray to your ancestors to ask for help in everyday situations and concerns. Make their favorite dish to thank them. Learn about their hometown and the customs they practiced. Learn their language. Ask them for support and guidance. Invite them to cook and eat with you. Invite them to visit you in your dreams. Ask them to help you with your gardening or any other work, craft, or hobby. Invoke them when doing magical work. Connecting to your ancestors will help you feel more grounded.

Saints

I first want to get one thing out of the way. You do not have to be Catholic or Christian to work with saints. Nor are all saints Catholic or Christian.

Saints are people who once lived and, during their life here on earth, consistently performed great miracles that could not be explained away as coincidences.

Let me rephrase what I just said. Saints are magicians who once lived and, during their life here on earth, consistently performed great manifestations or spells that could not be explained away as coincidences.

Saints continue to perform miracles even after their death. I can honestly say without reservation that I have never had a petition to a saint go unanswered. I may not always obtain the result I wanted, but I have never been left with my prayer unanswered.

The relationship Italian witchcraft practitioners have with the saints they work with has its own particularities. Saints are not viewed as gods. They are viewed as equals, but saints have the advantage of having the ability to intercede on our behalf. They are the practitioner's influential friend who has God's, Jesus's, or the Blessed Virgin Mary's ear. They are tasked with taking the practitioner's concerns to their attention and obtaining the results requested. Here's where it gets interesting. If the saint is performing, they are showered with love and devotion. This is best illustrated by the traditional custom of the Saint Joseph Day altar. The original custom from Sicily and Campania used to be that the size of the altar and the quantity of food offerings were commensurate with the harvest of the previous year. If a family was happy with the previous year's harvest, Saint Joseph's altar would reflect that. If a family was somewhat happy, their altar would boast fewer offerings. If a family was very dissatisfied with their harvest, they may not celebrate Saint Joseph's day at all.

This withholding of the love (and offerings) is called saint punishing. It was very common for my grandmother's generation, and those before her generation, to threaten and punish saints that were not pulling their weight, so to speak. Threatening consisted of just that, threats. They would utter threats at the saint in the same breath they petitioned them. They began with petitioning the saint for a favor and ended the prayer or ritual by threatening: "Make it happen, or else you're dead to me." If threats didn't work, they punished their saints. Punishing ranged from mild, such as not placing fresh flowers in front of their portraits or statues, to moderate, such as taking the statue or portrait and wrapping it in a black cloth and shoving it in a drawer. In extreme cases, a practitioner would go as far as defacing, disrespecting, or even burning the portrait or statue. When my Zia Paolina would put away portraits and statues to punish a saint, she would make sure to tell the saint she was sore at that they'd been replaced and with whom. If, after punishing the saint, something occurred that made them think that their saint had come through for them, all was forgiven and forgotten. The statue or portrait would come out of its dark drawer cell. It would be cleansed and polished and put back in its original place of honor— or an even better location in the home. There would be offerings of a celebratory meal, fresh flowers, sweets, and cash, and all would be well in the world. Quite a contrast from religious or pious devotion to saints, no?

How about a more mainstream example? If you're reading my book, I'm willing to bet you've seen or at least heard of the Saint Joseph Real Estate (Spell) Kit. If not, don't worry; I will explain. This kit is widely available. It is sold at Catholic supply stores, on Amazon.com, and other places for the sole purpose of helping with selling homes. No matter what brand of kit you buy, the instructions are all the same. The kit comes with a prayer and a statue of Saint Joseph. You bury the statue in the ground, upside down and facing your home. Once your home sells, you then dig it up, clean it, and put the statue in a place of honor in your new home. This prayer—no, let's call it what it really is—this saint punishing kit works. Period.

Each village in Italy had its patron saints that immigrants brought to the new world. Each family had its patron saints on top of their village patrons. For example, in my family, the village patron is Sant' Eustachio (Saint Eustace), but my family's patron is Sant' Antonio di Padova (Saint Anthony of Padua). I have relatives whose village saint is San Gennaro (Saint Januarius), but the family patron is Saint Barbara. Family patrons are saints that have a proven track record of consistently coming through for a family in all matters—not just what the saint is known for. Saint Anthony is best known as finder of lost souls, lost people, lost items, and a long list of other things. However, in my family, Saint Anthony is the go-to guy for everything, especially matters pertaining to health and children. That is what makes him our patron.

How to Start a Relationship and Work with Saints

Pick a saint. You can pick based on previous knowledge of them or based on your need. For example, you may choose a saint your nonna was devoted to or a saint known for granting the favor you wish to obtain—for example, you'd like a good spouse. You do your research or ask someone knowledgeable for a recommendation. After research-ing the saints most known for helping people find a good spouse, you decide on Saint Therese of Lisieux. Research this saint. Learn every-thing you can about her like you would a person you wanted to get to know. Obtain a prayer card or print her image off the Internet. Find out what she likes and make offerings to her.

When I started out, I had a book of novenas and a copy of *Lives of the Saints*. I would look up saints by what my needs were and learn more about them by looking up their lives. I would choose the saint I worked with based on whether I felt an affinity toward them because of who they were, over whether they were best known for granting the favor I needed. This method has served me well. I have had the best results working with saints based on this criterion over choosing a saint because they are known for granting the favor I need.

Here is an ancient list of saints for common needs given to me by my Zia Paolina:

Desperate situations: Saint Gregory Taumaturgo

For a good death: Saint Joseph, spouse of the Blessed Virgin Mary

For rain and for shine (to change the weather): Saint Agabio, Saint Grato, and Saint Genoveffa (Geneviève)

Safe and happy birth: Saint Anne, mother of the Blessed Virgin Mary

To die with safe passage to heaven: Saint Ursula

To find lost objects: Saint Anthony of Padua

To have children: Saint Francis of Paola

Travel by land: The Holy Magi (The Three Wise Men)

Travel by sea: Saint Francis Xavier

Here is an ancient list of arts, professions, and trades and their patron saints, given to me by my Zia Paolina:

Archers: Saint Sebastian

Blacksmiths: Saint Peter of Vincoli

Coach builders: Saint Eligio

Cooks: Saint Lawrence

Gardeners: Saint Urban

Glaziers: Saint Giacomo Allemano and Saint Nicolo

Goldsmiths: Saint Dunstano

Hoteliers: Saint Teodoto

Hunters: Saint Eustace

Lawyers: Saint Ivone and Saint Andrea Avellino

Maids (housekeepers): Saint Zita

Masons: *Quattro Coronati* (The Four Crowned Saints)—Saint Sinforiano, Saint Claudio, Saint Nicostrato, and Saint Castorio. According to tradition, these four Christian stonecutters suffered martyrdom under the empire of Diocletian.

Musicians: Saint Cecilia

Navigators: Saint Nicolo and Saint Peter Gonzales

Notaries: Saint John

Painters: Saint Lucas and Saint Lazarus

Pharmacists: Saints Cosmo and Damiano

Philosophers: Saint Catherine

Physicians: Saints Cosmo and Damiano

Printers: Saint John of God, Saint John Evangelist

Scholars: Saint Nicolo

Shepherds: Saint Genoveffa (Genevieve)

Shoemakers: Saint Crispin and Saint Aniano

Soldiers: Saint George

Surgeons: Saints Cosmo and Damiano

Tailors: Saint Omobono

Travelers: Saint Julian l'Ospitaliere

With the Internet, all this information is instantly available at our fingertips. However, the work of discerning which saint is best for your work and how to approach them remains the same. That information isn't always on the Internet. One book I highly recommend for researching and picking saints to work with is the *Encyclopedia of Mystics, Saints & Sages* by Judika Illes. This book is specifically geared toward the practitioner of saint magic. As the title suggests, it contains saints from a variety of religious traditions, not just Catholic or Christian. Each entry contains pertinent facts about each saint's history and how to go about petitioning them for your magical work.

Saint Anthony of Padua: Finder of Lost Objects

Saint Anthony is known worldwide by Catholics and non-Catholics as the saint to call upon for lost objects. If you are American, you may already be very familiar with this prayer to Saint Anthony:

> "Tony, Tony, come on down. Something is lost and must be found!"

Long before learning "Tony, Tony, come on down," I was taught a different way to request his help.

Saint Anthony happens to be my family's patron saint. He does not have to be your family's patron in order for him to become yours or your family's. All that is required is that you open a spiritual dialogue with him. Get to know him. Work with him. That is how these relationships are forged.

This is the legend of Saint Anthony told to me many years ago.

Saint Anthony and Ezzelino di Romano, a cruel tyrant and feudal lord, were contemporaries. The story goes that it was, in fact, Saint Anthony who aided Ezzelino di Romano in finding his lost inner peace, thus making him repent all his past acts of cruelty.

Saint Anthony was in a Franciscan monastery in Padua (Italy), and people would seek him out to get back their lost inner peace, lost serenity, and lost love, with great success.

One day, the Provincial Father of the Franciscan monastery had lost a magnificent antique painting of great value. He went to Saint Anthony and said to him, "You who grant people back their inner peace and tranquility, can you please tell me what to do to find lost objects?"

Saint Anthony instructed him to "pray to God before going to bed, and tomorrow, tell me about what you dreamt."

The Provincial superior did what the saint instructed him to do, and found the painting that now hangs in the Basilica of Saint Anthony in Padua. From that day forward, Saint Anthony also became the finder of lost objects. Here is what you need to do to petition his help.

At night, before going to bed, pray to God and then recite this verse:

Antonio a Padova nato

E da tutti adorato

Stanotte faccio vuto

Pe n'oggetto perduto

Sant'Antonio putente,

Me teniteme in mente

E nsuonno me dicite

Chelle che po vulite

Pe dirme c'aggia fa,

Pe la cosa truvà.

Anthony born in Padua

And adored by all

Tonight, I make a *voto* (promise/vow/offering)

For a lost object

Powerful Saint Anthony

Keep me in mind

Tell me in my sleep

What you want (in return)

For telling me what I must do

To find this thing.

That night, the person who prayed will have dreams that symbolize what Saint Anthony requests from them. The following night the person will pray the same prayer, now vowing to Saint Anthony to keep their promise and carry out his request, such as making a religious offering (ex-voto) or donating money to charity. That night the person will dream a new dream, and the symbolism will direct them to the lost object.

The prayer states, "Anthony born in Padua." Saint Anthony was, in fact, born in Lisbon, Portugal. Bear in mind that I was taught this legend and prayer forty years ago and, at that time, was told it was at least over a hundred years old. Prayers to saints, specifically folk prayers, typically began with "Saint _____ born in _____" or "Saint ____ from _____." These types of prayers were, in fact, incantations largely composed by laypeople and handed down orally.

Saint Anthony is a powerful saint. He is the finder (and revealer) of all things lost: mundane, arcane, sacred, and profane. The following are examples to explain what I mean:

Mundane: Everyday objects such as keys.

Arcane: Motivation. Purpose. Hidden agenda.

Sacred: Grace. Inner peace. Connection to God.

Profane: Intuition. Clairvoyance. Magical power. Adversary's Achilles heel.

I have already explained the sacred (inner peace) and the mundane (lost painting) with the telling of the legend.

An example of the arcane would be to call on Saint Anthony to reveal to us another person's motivation or hidden agenda. Or, perhaps we lack motivation and wish Saint Anthony to help us find it.

Profane means that Saint Anthony can be called upon for magical work. Examples would be to help you find a mago/maga (sorcerer) that you can trust to seek out a service. Another is to request he reveal to you who your enemies are and what their weaknesses are.

Saint Anthony is also a giver. This means that no prayer to Saint Anthony goes unanswered. He will always give you something. It may not be exactly what you asked for, but it will definitely be what you need.

When I feel overwhelmed by a situation, I always ask Saint Anthony to help me find clarity. He always delivers.

What kinds of promises and offerings does Saint Anthony like? He loves offerings that mirror his work. If he helps you "find" something, do the same for people in your midst.

Saint Anthony's Feast Day is June 13. This is the reason that many Italians (especially people from Naples) view the number thirteen as lucky. When I was growing up, and on a smaller scale today, in Italian parishes in America and Canada, it was customary to throw a big block party with games, rides, and many food vendors. Today, many of us continue to celebrate in our homes by inviting family and friends and preparing the same food we enjoyed at these feasts. Pizza fritta (fried pizza dough, sweet or savory), panino (bun) stuffed with pork sausage and fried peppers, and cannoli (pastry tubes filled with a ricotta cream) are some examples.

If you want to begin working with Saint Anthony, all you need to do is ask him to help you find things: parking spots, the right friends, the solution to a problem, and so on. At times, his response is instant and literal. Other times, he will send you a message in your thoughts or dreams, and you will have to work a bit to decode it.

Another point I want to make is that what you request doesn't have to literally be something you lost. It can be something you wish to find.

One last thing: There are times when I have lost (or thrown out or given away) an object knowing full well that it was lost forever because I remember where it was lost and it is irretrievable. These were objects of tremendous sentimental value, so I was completely heartbroken. On these occasions, I have prayed to Saint Anthony. Much to my astonishment, I have experienced the following miracles:

The object magically reappeared where I normally stored it, even though I remember losing it.

I was gifted (not mine, but) the exact same object by someone who (a) didn't know I had and lost the same object and (b) had no idea why they were giving one to me, but they just "thought of me" when they saw it.

Having put the lost object out of my mind, I found the same object in a thrift store and/or online auction site (on a couple of occasions, I could identify it as previously mine!).

And lastly, when the object was lost for good and could not be found, Saint Anthony helped me find peace.

Madonna

The summer I turned seventeen, I went to see a Sicilian psychic recommended by a friend. I had had my cards read many times by shopping mall fortune-tellers, but none of that prepared me for this experience.

This psychic called herself Marina (of course, not her real name). Marina couldn't have been more than twenty-five years old. She had large, dark, almond-shaped eyes, a deep olive complexion, and a thick mane of raven hair that she wore in a loose bun. She had both a mesmerizing and comforting presence. She lived in a little house in the heart of Little Italy. Across the street was the church of Our Lady of Defense, where my parents had been married almost thirty years prior.

The scent of candles burning, church incense, and marinara sauce wafted out an open window to the right of her front door. I rang the bell and she let me in. Marina received clients in a little room to the right of the front entrance of her home. It was a sparsely furnished little room. There was a little table with a red table cover and two chairs. In the corner was another little table with at least a dozen statues of various saints and candles burning. On the table with the red cover sat a Bible, rosary, and a deck of tarot cards. The plaster walls and ceiling were painted stark white. A single light bulb hung from the ceiling from a cord. On one wall hung a very worn crucifix, on another a framed portrait of the Sacred Heart of Jesus, on another wall a portrait of the Madonna, and on the fourth wall was a little window facing the street with a white lace curtain. Above the window was a broken horseshoe with a red ribbon tied around it. Having grown up in an Italian Roman Catholic household, I found these portraits and statues familiar and comforting. The scent of church incense candles burning outside of church was intriguing. The presence of a deck of tarot cards on the same table as a Bible and rosary—now that was completely alien.

She moved the table aside and placed the two chairs facing each other. She opened a box of table salt and poured it onto the floor, creating a white circle surrounding the chairs. She then invited me to carefully step into the circle and sit on one of the chairs. We sat facing each other, toes to toes, knees to knees. After blessing us both with holy water, she took my hands into hers and gripped them tightly. She then closed her eyes and threw her head back. She recited a short prayer and then began to speak . . . very quickly as though she was afraid of running out of time. Marina told me things about myself only I knew. She told me of my past and present as though she lived it herself. She knew so much about me and what I held in my heart, and she did so without using her cards. She then spoke of a future that seemed so outrageous to me in my inexperience and current situation that I quickly dismissed it as nonsense. Although now, thirty years later, I can assure you that, much to my amazement, it ALL came to pass. Lastly, she told me I was cursed and that she could help. My lack of reaction to her pronouncement that I was cursed intrigued her. She asked me, "Did you hear what I said?" "Yes," I replied. "You are not surprised?" asked Marina. "No," I replied. "How are you not surprised or even afraid?" "You just finished telling me my past and present less than five minutes ago. If all that doesn't sound cursed to you, I don't know what is." "And you are not afraid?" "Of what? That I may be cursed? Nah, I'm used to it." I paid the lady her thirty dollars, which she instructed me to place inside her Bible. I carefully stepped over the ring of salt and I left.

I was grateful for the long bus ride home, for it gave me a chance to be alone with my thoughts. I sat in my favorite seat at the back of the bus with the window on my right. I slid the window open as far as it would go and leaned my head against the window frame. My reading by Marina swirled in my head. I needed to know how she read for me without using cards. I needed to know more about the ring of salt and how she knew so much about me just from holding my hands. I needed to know the prayer she recited before she began. I needed to learn how to do what she did more than I'd ever wanted or needed anything in my life.

Sometime that same week or maybe it was a couple of weeks later—it was so long ago, it seemed like it could have been the same day—I bumped into my friend Marco on my way home from the bus stop. Marco was on his way to his Nonna Filomena's house. Marco's Nonna

Filomena lived alone. Marco would visit her every other day or so in case she needed something. Instead of going our separate ways at the intersection, he invited me to go with him, and I accepted. It is 'scustumato (very poor manners) to decline visiting someone's nonna, and Marco's nonna's black pepper taralli were famous in my neighborhood. When Marco and I arrived, Nonna Filomena was frying up some broccoli rabe in olive oil and garlic. She was barely five feet tall and couldn't have been ninety pounds soaking wet. She had her beautiful stark-white hair in a bun and wore a scarf around her head that matched the full apron she wore over her house dress. Marco and I approached Nonna Filomena to greet her with the customary kiss on each cheek. When I approached her kitchen, a plain old drinking glass that was sitting in her sink spontaneously shattered.

Nonna Filomena, in one smooth motion, turned off the stove and grabbed me by the left wrist, glared at me, and asked in her native Neapolitan dialect: "Where have you been?"

"Nowhere?" I replied.

"Don't think you can take me for a ride. I will ask you again: Where have you been?"

At this point, Marco, mortified by his nonna's behavior, tried to intervene. Nonna Filomena shoved all six feet and 180 pounds of him several feet with her left hand while maintaining her viselike grip on my left wrist with her right. She fixed her eyes on me and said, "When glass spontaneously shatters, it means there is a witch nearby. Since neither of you kids are witches, then one of you . . . you went to see one and she put a curse on you."

"I did go to have my future told," and before I could finish that sentence, Nonna Filomena, still maintaining her powerful grip on my left wrist, instructed me to pick a walnut with my right hand from the bowl on the kitchen counter. She took the walnut from me with her left hand and slammed it on the kitchen counter. She then opened her hand and showed it to me. The walnut shell was perfectly cracked open, and inside it was all black and shriveled.

Nonna Filomena finally let go of my wrist. She grabbed a large leaf from her grape vine. She placed the black, shriveled walnut in the center of the leaf. She then slapped me across the face so hard that tears instantly sprung and poured from my eyes. She took a napkin and wiped the tears from my face and placed the napkin in the grape leaf. Then she instructed me to spit on the walnut three times, and after I did that, she shoved a clove of garlic in my mouth and made me swallow it whole "to send Saint Michael to kill the devil the witch put inside me." She tied up the leaf, making a little bundle, and tossed it in the fire burning in her fireplace. She then made me (and Marco) pray the rosary with her while the bundle burned.

When the bundle was done burning and we were done praying, Nonna Filomena fixed us a plate of broccoli rabe and brought out her famous black pepper taralli.

When it was time for us to go, Nonna Filomena placed her open hand on my cheek and said to me, "Don't worry; everything is okay now. Tell me, who is your Madonna?"

"What do you mean?" I asked.

"Who is your Madonna? Which Madonna do you pray to?"

"Isn't there only one? At church, there is only one."

Nonna Filomena fished a small card out of her apron pocket and handed it to me. It was a holy card of La Madonna del Carmine (Our Lady of Mount Carmel).

"Pfft, church! What does church know? This is my Madonna. It is she that sent you to me to be released from the spell that witch cast on you. Pray to her to thank her and that she keep you safe, you stupid kid."

Different Madonnas

The Madonna is the one and only Virgin Mary, Mother of Jesus. Why are there so many different Madonnas? There is a Madonna for every aspect of the Virgin Mary: Our Lady of Immaculate Conception is the aspect of the Virgin Mother, Our Lady of Perpetual Help is the aspect of the Virgin Mary that answers our prayers for help, and so on. Then, we have the Madonnas named for the geographical locations where her apparitions were witnessed: Our Lady of Mount Carmel, Our Lady of Lourdes, Our Lady of Medjugorje, etc.

Then there is the personal Madonna. The personal Madonna is the characterization of the devotee's chosen aspect of the Madonna that is informed by the personal relationship the devotee shares with their Madonna.

Personal Madonna

The personal Madonna is a concept that is so simple yet at the same time very complex. The reason is that, unlike previous generations of our ancestors who lived their lives in small towns, inherited an oral tradition, and didn't question it, we have unlimited access to information via the Internet and are plagued by the need to neatly define, explain, and categorize things that are best left to simply "be."

The Virgin Mary, Saint Mary, la Madonna, Queen of Heaven, and so on—her names and representations are endless in various religions, art, cultures, and geographical locations. Despite her many names and faces, Mary is ONE and She is Mother.

One thing every matriarch and patriarch in my family and community had in common was their relationship and devotion to la Madonna. This relationship and devotion are completely independent of religion. Every Mary devotee is devoted to their own Personal Madonna whether or not they believe in anything else. As I spoke to more and more people, I began to understand that each person's relationship with Mary is informed by who they need their Mother to be.

In this example, all five of these people are devoted to La Madonna del Carmine (Our Lady of Mount Carmel):

Zia Sylvia's Madonna was who she turned to for comfort. She was maternal and nurturing—like she wished her mother had been. Zia Sylvia often felt helpless, and she turned to her Mother for comfort.

Commara Lina's Madonna was a healer. She invoked la Madonna to work through her when she placed her hands on people who came to her for healing.

Zio Giuseppe believed his crops were at the whim of his Madonna. He made sure to keep a meticulous flower bed surrounding her statue in the front of his home. He kept her statue clean and in good repair, and he tended her flower garden with great care to make sure she was happy. When his Madonna was happy, she sent good weather and his vegetable crops flourished. If he failed to maintain her flower garden and let weeds grow rampant, she sent pests to invade his vegetable garden.

Zia Paolina's Madonna was vengeful and destructive. Her Madonna protected and defended her in all her endeavors without prejudice. One day Zia Paolina invoked her for defense against evil, and the next day she would invoke her for retaliation (cursing) against those who meant her harm. On the occasion that Zia Paolina was not happy with her Madonna, she would hold a lit cigarette to the eyes on a portrait or prayer card of La Madonna del Carmine. When my Zia went blind from diabetes, she said she had it coming. As far as Zia Paolina was concerned, the Madonna was (rightfully) exacting vengeance for all the times she burned her eyes out.

My neighbor Isabella's Madonna was the decision maker. Her Madonna dictated all outcomes. Something would happen or not happen at the hands of her Madonna. If she had a decision to make, she would ask her Madonna to give her a sign and that is what she would decide—even if she disagreed with the decision, because her belief was "Mother knows best."

Your Personal Madonna

If you grew up Catholic and you feel comfortable working with la Madonna, great! If not, don't worry. It does not mean you don't have a Personal Madonna. We all have a spirit Mother. Feel free to call her what feels right to you.

Roman Deities

Many stregoneria practitioners venerate Roman deities as well as saints. Unlike saints, Roman deities never lived as humans. Their place in the hierarchy is somewhere between saints and the Blessed Virgin. Practitioners are very specific with what is the domain of Roman gods versus saints, versus the Blessed Virgin, versus The Holy Trinity. It is not uncommon to work with a combination of gods and saints to obtain a goal. This is evident in spells that must be performed on a specific day of the week, using the color and metal of the Roman god ruling that day, but also reciting an incantation to a saint and the Blessed Virgin.

The process of developing a relationship and working with Roman deities is very like how we work with and relate to saints. It is best not to hop from god to god. Pick one based on your affinity to them. Learn about them. Get to know them. Work with them. The more you work with them, the stronger your relationship and the better your results.

I work mainly with Diana and Venus. I work with Diana for matters of my home and family, including pets. I work with Venus for matters of my personal life, health, and career. Diana is my family's patron, and Venus is mine. I can't even tell you how or why this came to be; it just always has been. My dad's patron was Bacchus. When I give this some thought, it occurs to me that this may have been because my dad wished he could relax and enjoy life a little more than he did. When good things happened to him, he always attributed his good fortune to Bacchus.

Fairies

Fairies are what we called the spirits that lived in the garden and house plants. If our house and garden fairies are appeased, our plants thrive. We don't really work with fairies; we take care of their homes. I guess, now that I come to think of it, we serve them. Huh.

Animal Spirits

Animal spirits are different from all other spirits in the sense that they seek us out. The type of magical work we do attracts certain animal spirits. We can also choose to work with an animal spirit when we want to invoke a certain animal's qualities. I am allergic to cats, yet cats are drawn to me like I am walking catnip. Crows and ravens appear and acknowledge me everywhere I go, and I feel a profound kinship and comfort in their presence. I have had a dog spirit with me since I was a child and long before having dogs of my own that have crossed over. I see some marmots on the side of the road and go out of my mind with joy. There are animals I have a paralyzing fear of, however, such as snakes, spiders, and scorpions.

I'm willing to bet you have animals that are drawn to you and animals you are drawn to as well as animals you are afraid of. These relationships all have something to teach us.

To understand these relationships better, begin by taking a sheet of paper. Then make three lists: the animals you are drawn to, the animals that are drawn to you, and the animals you are deathly afraid of.

The animals you are drawn to are your animal spirit kin. They are animals that have been by your side through many lifetimes.

The animals that are drawn to you are your teachers. They are drawn to you to teach you who you are. Study their qualities, and you will find these same qualities lie inside you.

The animals you are deathly afraid of have qualities that lie dormant inside you, qualities within yourself that frighten you.

Elemental Spirits

Our planet is made up of four elements: air, earth, fire, and water. Each element has a spirit. These spirits are powerful and may be unpredictable. It takes a lot of work . . . and . . . caution to develop a working relationship with these powerful forces of nature. To develop a relationship with elemental spirits, begin by inviting them into your home.

Air: Open your windows daily to air out your home. When you do so, welcome the spirit of air. Feel the energy in your home lighten almost immediately. All it takes is a few minutes.

Earth: The spirit of earth is in everything that comes from the earth. The spirit of earth neutralizes and banishes all negative energies and evil spirits. When we use salt to purify, we are working with the spirit of earth. When we bury something in the ground to neutralize or bind it, we are working with the spirit of earth.

Fire: The spirit of fire is extremely excitable, volatile, and unpredictable. When we burn candles, we are working with the spirit of fire. Always exercise caution when working with the spirit of fire. You may light up a charcoal disc to burn a little incense, and next thing you know, the fire department is putting out a fire that is gutting your home.

When working with fire, stay calm and always have a fire extinguisher nearby. I say stay calm because the spirit of fire feeds off our emotions—good and bad. When I was growing up, everyone had a working hearth. During family get-togethers when the energy was high, the fire in the fireplace roared and popped like crazy. An uncle always had to tend to it and subdue it a bit with ash (spirit of earth). The spirit of fire also communicates with us through its flames. My friend's mom would read the fire in her hearth the way someone else would read cards.

Water: Take a shower. After you are done washing, linger a little longer. You will suddenly feel a tremendous calm wash over you. This is your body and mind surrendering to the spirit of water. This state of mind permits inspiration to flow freely. Make note of any thoughts that cross your mind while you are communing with the spirit of water. They are messages from the spirit of water. The spirit of water also opens you up to communication with the dead. If you are a person who is under a lot of stress or suffer from chronic anxiety, communing with the spirit of water in a bath, shower, swimming pool, natural body of water, or rain is very soothing and beneficial.

To develop a working relationship with any elemental spirit, you need to work with them to get to know them. Be patient with them and yourself. Start with one at a time. Spirits are like us in the sense that we will be more compatible with some than others. Work with the ones you hit it off with right away and work with them often. This will build your confidence, and you will create easily and effortlessly.

Culto dei morti (Worship of the Dead)

Signora Teresa, a beloved personage who lived on the outskirts of Naples, Italy, died peacefully in her sleep in the summer of 1965 during a record-breaking heat wave just ten days shy of her one hundredth birthday. In life, she was known to bring good luck to young ladies wanting to find a good husband. Signora Teresa was a renowned seamstress who, in her later years, taught sewing in her hometown.

Signora Teresa would always say, "If you girls want a man to fall in love with you, all you have to do his feed him basil." When the young ladies were done giggling, she would continue: "Pork sausage made from a pig slaughtered on the full moon, seasoned with garlic and dried basil, salt and pepper, and beautifully browned in a pan or on the grill, served with a salad of tomatoes, cucumbers, and onions tossed in good olive oil and topped with fresh basil cut in ribbons. Make sure to bake a fresh loaf of crusty bread to go with that, and a little homemade wine doesn't hurt. Don't forget to put garlic in the sausage, in case he's no good for you. If he's good for you and has good intentions, the basil will make him fall in love with you. If he's no good for you or does not have good intentions, the garlic will drive him away."

On the first anniversary of her death, her daughter had her body exhumed, as is customary in this part of Italy, lovingly washed Signora Teresa's remains, and clothed her in a new dress. Women from all around, who over the years had gone to Signora Teresa for help finding a good husband, descended upon the cemetery and placed an offering in the ground surrounding her grave. Hopeful women wanting to find a good husband would visit her grave and pray to her. When they married, they would bring Signora Teresa a **bonbonniere** or their wedding bouquet as a thank you.

This is the story my Zia Tina told us when we became "of age" in the 1970s and '80s to start "thinking about finding a nice boy to settle down with." "Pray to Signora Teresa that you meet a nice boy. Just before leaving for a date with a boy, say a prayer to Signora Teresa that if he is the right one, he falls in love with you; if he is wrong for you or bad news, he go away. Carry a basil leaf and a clove of garlic in your purse." My cousins who prayed to Signora Teresa swear up and down that it is thanks to her that they have good husbands. Zia Tina, disappointed that I dismissed praying to a regular person I never met because she had died before I was born and whom I had never even seen a picture of and thought of as a silly superstition, announced to me that she had to take matters into her own hands when she saw "I was throwing my life away." She claimed that she prayed to Signora Teresa on my behalf: "See how Signora Teresa got rid of the no good and sent you a good man?"

Praying to ordinary dead people was more common than praying to God and saints among our ancestors and as recently as my parents' generation.

Mothers prayed to their dead mothers for guidance and to help them in affairs of the family. Widows prayed to their late husbands to continue to watch over and guide the family. Widowers prayed to their dead wives for help with raising their family. People (especially from Naples) prayed to the souls in purgatory for the winning lotto numbers. People who were wronged prayed to their ancestors and the souls in purgatory for justice (although they really meant vengeance). Sorcerers/sorceresses invoked their ancestors and/or the souls in purgatory to thwart, harm, or curse their rivals.

Once the shock of the loss and the period of intense grieving has subsided, the departed family member rejoins the family, only now in spirit form. The best way I can describe this transition is that their body dies and they completely leave us for as long as it takes for us to become accustomed to the loss of their physicality. The belief is that our departed family members are still very interested in our day-to-day lives but now, being dead, have foreknowledge and the ability to intervene on our behalf from the hereafter, thus affecting the physical world.

We pray directly to our deceased loved ones for our day-to-day needs. Ironically, in turn, we pray for their souls' eternal rest. We maintain shrines in their honor in our homes. We pay money to the church to have Masses celebrated on their behalf.

Just like my parents and grandparents before me, I talk to my deceased loved ones all the time. I ask for all kinds of guidance, and you know what? I receive it. It may come as a quiet thought that crosses my mind or a vivid dream. They communicate with us indirectly through the words and actions of other people. The most interesting thing is how they pass on their talents to us.

I know I talked about this in an earlier chapter but, it never gets old for me. Here is another little example of what I mean. My mom was talented with textiles—knitting, crocheting, embroidery, and so on. I could only crochet a little. Suddenly, since my mom passed away in 2012, I now can do things with textiles far beyond my personal skill level, provided I have time to do so. When I have had the time, I have made beautiful things that I don't even know how I made them, considering my beginner's skill level—like magic. Stop. Of course, I believe in magic and that my mother is present and helping me create beautiful things. I wouldn't be writing this book if I didn't.

Other ways your deceased relatives communicate with you is by sending you gifts. Often these gifts appear on their birthdays or the anniversary of their death. Examples of gifts are:

You turn on the radio, and their favorite song is playing.

You're looking for something in your home and come across something they gave you that you haven't thought of or seen in ages.

You are suddenly inspired to cook their signature dish, and all the ingredients are on sale at the supermarket.

Someone gives you something, saying, "I had this thing. I never use it and I thought of you." It turns out to be something you really wanted, and the first person to pop in your mind is your deceased loved one.

You go to a thrift store, and the first thing you see is an object that reminds you of them, and it is something you have wanted for a while but haven't been actively thinking about. I've had this experience a few times, and since there wasn't a price tag on it, the clerk gave it to me.

You're browsing an Internet auction site and come across a bottle of the perfume they wore and you associate with them, that has long been discontinued, at an amazing price. I collect vintage perfume, specifically perfume that I associate with my loved ones, so this example is a little specific to me.

You can even ask for gifts. Seriously, just like I described to ask your angels for gifts. You will be amazed and awed by what they send you.

Coincidentally, as I was writing this chapter, my eldest daughter came to me with an object she found in an empty drawer in the basement. She showed it to me and said, "I brought you something." I looked down at the flat, rounded, triangular object the size of a quarter on her palm. "That is a guitar pick. As a matter of fact, it was your Nonno's guitar pick. That's him saying hello." This may seem a bit contrived to you reading this, but I am the person who emptied the drawer, and this guitar pick would not have been left in an empty dresser drawer by accident because I keep all my picks in a trinket box near my late dad's guitar.

We continue to interact with our dead in our daily lives; however, there are rules. For the first year after someone dies, it is expected that we do our best to not bother them by complaining to them nor ask them for anything except for them to send us a sign that they arrived okay. In fact, it is customary for a conversation to take place between family members that when they die, they promise to send a sign they arrived okay and that they visit whenever they can. In return, we pray for their souls in purgatory. We ask for God to have mercy on their souls and that their sins be forgiven and that when they are done serving their time in purgatory and are promoted to paradise, they are returned to us (in spirit). Although we do not ask them for anything the first year post-death, the deceased can ask us for things.

The focus is on making sure not to do anything that will displease the dead because we want them to feel positively toward us and be invested in our safety and success. The belief is that they can affect our lives both positively and negatively, and no one wants their dead messing up their lives. This is why it is taboo to speak ill of the dead. That and the fact that any ill we speak of them is like a negative reference and can hinder their progression out of purgatory or, worse, result in their being assigned to hell, from where they will exact their revenge by cursing us and ruining our lives. We have all seen how the most despicable person is elevated to sainthood by the same family members they were abusive or cruel to. This behavior is so common that it has become cliché in movies featuring Italians. There is usually a character who is a widow, and when her late husband is mentioned, she and everyone in the room do the sign of the cross and gaze upward saying, "He was a saint, may he rest in peace."

Incantation to Dream of the Deceased

Buon'anima buona, buon'anima cara/caro,

Non mi fa aspettare,

Buon'anima buona, buon'anima cara/caro

Buon'anima di _____,

Vien' a mi trovare!

Good good soul, dear good soul,

Don't make me wait,

Good soul of (insert name),

Come to visit me.

Buon'anima literally translates to *good soul*. It is the term used in conjunction with the name of the deceased the same way we use the word *late*.

I have personally experienced a significant amount of loss, and therefore, I have had many opportunities to test these beliefs. When they work, and they always do, I marvel at the result as if I am experiencing it for the first time. It never gets old.

The first dream of a deceased loved one often takes place in a large dining hall. There are many other identical tables meticulously arranged, each covered in a white tablecloth. There are other people sitting at various tables that you may or may not know. If you see other people you know, like acquaintances sitting at their own table with their deceased, they will not interact with you. I've had an experience or two where the person I knew made eye contact with me, and then we quickly went on with our personal business at hand. The only person that will interact with you is the most recently departed that you requested to visit you. You will be sitting at a small table with your deceased relative. They may look exactly as they did before they died or, especially in the case of people who die from cancer or other long illnesses, they will appear full of vitality and health and often significantly younger than you expect. They arrive immaculately dressed and with the distracted air of a person being pulled away from a wonderful vacation and at the same time with a sense of urgency to return from where they were. The visit is brief but leaves the living with a sense of peace that their loved one has arrived safe and sound. Subsequent visits may be via dreams, a scent in the air you associate with the person, gifts, and so on.

If you are not already experiencing connection and a day-to-day communication with your dead, begin by telling yourself that you will be on the lookout for signs. When you see or experience something that you think may be a sign, say "thank you" and write it down in a place reserved for this data collection. At first, it may be really small things. Do not dismiss these little things by explaining them logically. Keep your magical mind open. By keeping your believing spirit open, these little things will quickly become bigger things that you won't be able to easily explain logically.

In Italian, we say, "Provare per credere," which is the Italian version of "Seeing is believing," except the Italian phrase has a nuance that is absent in the English phrase. Provare per credere invites us to try something, and when we experience it for ourselves, we will believe.

Chapter 14

The Sacred and the Profane

Elements of Catholicism in the Practice of Italian Witchcraft

Italian Americans have long been defined by their religious beliefs and practices. During the great wave of immigration, the Irish-dominated Roman Catholic hierarchy identified Italian immigrants as the "Italian problem" and mere "sacramental Catholics" due to the latter's popular anti-clericalism, the seamless blending of witch-craft and ecclesiastic teachings, their deep devotion to the cult of the saints and the Virgin Mary, and the spectacularly staged feste that mixed the sacred and the profane in streets across America. During the 20th century, Italian American spirituality and religious prac-tices have undergone significant transformations with shifts in theo-logical tenets, economic status, and the political climate.

—John D. Calandra, Italian American Institute and The Italian American Studies Program of Queens College

The practice of Italian witchcraft—stregoneria, folk magic, folk healing, whatever you choose to call it—is condemned by the Roman Catholic Church. However, every single practitioner that taught me identified as Catholic. Even I identify as Catholic although I haven't set foot in a church to attend mass since attending a friend's mother's funeral mass almost fifteen years ago. The elders I learned from, women and men who were born in the late 19th and early 20th century, would never identify as or call themselves *streghe*. Streghe is what they called someone they feared was "putting the malocchio" or cursing them! The ones who practiced witchcraft as an occupation called themselves **maga** (sorceress) or **mago** (magician).

If you were raised Italian Catholic, these elements of Catholicism will resonate with you more strongly than for someone who was not raised Italian or Catholic. However, there are always exceptions on both sides. Maybe you were raised Irish Catholic, and therefore, the elements in Italian witchcraft make you feel uncomfortable. Don't use them. Maybe you were raised Jewish, but these Catholic elements make your heart sing. Then, by all means, use them.

Spirituality is how we express our relationship with the creative force of the universe. It is how we express our relationship with our creator, with God. You can have a full spiritual life with or without practicing an organized religion. You can practice a religion of your choice as well as a magical practice. The beauty of Italian witchcraft is that you can have it all. Culture, tradition, spirituality, and magic. The mundane, arcane, sacred, and profane.

Saints in Our Daily Lives

I touched on saints in our daily lives in the the previous chapter. Italian witchcraft has a strong element of saint magic. Saints play an important role in our daily lives. They are our confidants and partners in magic and prayer. They are present everywhere we turn. Statues, portraits, prayer cards, the names of the villages our ancestors came from, the charms we recite to cure a toothache, the Italian neighborhoods we grew up in, the tchotchkes hanging in our cars. How many times have you helped a friend who wasn't Catholic find a lost item by teaching them the prayer to Saint Anthony:

"Tony, Tony, come around, something's lost and can't be found."

And it worked.

Of course, it worked. It always works.

I've been saying it wrong my whole life, but I don't change the way I say it because it works. I taught my family the way I say it and it works for them:

"Tony, Tony, turn around, something's lost and must be found."

You are most likely named after a saint. Did you know that being named after a saint places you under that saint's protection, whether you even know who they are?

What I am saying is that your life is already full of saints—whether you know it or not.

Sacramentals

Sacramentals are very powerful Catholic symbols made into objects that can be used as tools in magical work. The same sacramentals used in the Catholic Church are used in blessing rituals, whereby the sacramentals are never disrespected. However, they are also used quite extensively in stregoneria (witchcraft) and that usage blends the sacred (sacramentals) with the profane (stregoneria).

Examples of sacramentals include:

Altars: We set up altars in our homes.

Ashes: Blessed palm from Palm Sunday is burned, and the ashes can be used for a variety of spells.

Bells: We rings a bell at the beginning and the end of a ritual.

Blessed medals: These are used as amulets and talismans.

Blessed palms: The blessed palm leaves are used in spells or burned to use the ash in spells.

Blessed salt: Common salt is exorcised and blessed by a priest. It is used in the blessing of holy water.

Blessing: This practice involves blessing people, animals, places, and objects.

Candles: Tapers, votives, or nine-day novena or memorial candles are used in spells and blessings. They also are used to communicate with spirits.

Cemeteries and mausoleums: Objects obtained from cemeteries and mausoleums are used in spells and spirit communication.

Church buildings and grounds: These are places of power where practitioners go to recharge and pray.

Cross: This symbol of the cross of crucifixion is used as a ward or talisman.

Crucifix: This symbol of the cross of crucifixion has the figure of Christ on it. The crucifix differs from the cross in that it has the body (or corpus) of Christ. It is a ward or talisman used in healing spells, exorcisms, and protection spells.

Exorcism: This sacrament is performed on a person believed to be a victim of demonic possession.

Ex-voto: This is an offering to a saint or deity to thank them for the miracle granted. An example is the public thank you to Saint Expedite when he grants a favor.

Fire: This symbol of the Holy Spirit is used to purify.

Holy oil: Holy oil is used in healing. It is applied to the body of the sick person.

Holy water: Holy water is water that has been mixed with exorcised salt and then blessed/exorcised by a priest. Technically, holy water cannot be purchased. What you are paying for is the bottle that contains it. Some practitioners make their own using a solution of plain water and salt to cleanse people and objects and reserve holy water to bless and protect against evil.

Icons: Icons are statues and portraits of Jesus, the Blessed Virgin, and saints.

Incense: Church incense is used to purify and bless the home.

Liturgical year: Certain spells are timed to be carried out during a specific time of the year.

Mary gardens: This feature in the front yard of a home consists of a statue of the Blessed Virgin surrounded by a flower garden.

Medal: A flat, round, or oval piece of metal on which an emblem or picture representing a devotion or object of veneration has been impressed, such as the image of a saint. Medals are inexpensive and easily obtained at Catholic supply shops. They are used as amulets and talismans.

Rosary: This closed chain of beads has a short tail of beads with a crucifix on the end. It is used to recite prayers in a specific sequence, collectively called the rosary. Praying the rosary is effective in removing and preventing affliction from malocchio, spells, and curses. Used as an amulet and talisman, it is a ward against malocchio. It can also be used in a curse. A rosary that once belonged to a deceased loved one can be used to connect with them.

Scapular: A devotional scapular is made of two small squares of cloth (wool) about two inches wide. On the square of wool is another cloth with the image of the Blessed Virgin on one side and the Sacred Heart of Jesus on the other. These cloth squares are connected by two strings and joined like a necklace with a square at either end. The scapular is worn so that one small square may rest on the back and the other on the breast when placed over one's head. They are used to make charm bags (santucci), talismans against malocchio, spells, and curses.

Sign of the cross: This is used in blessing, healing, prayer, and protection.

Wedding rings: These rings are used for spells and divination. They must be blessed.

Prayers

Novena prayers and psalms are often used as magic spells or in addition to incantations.

Pilgrimages to Places of Power

Religious or natural places of power are excellent for meditating and recharging. Practitioners will often bring things home from these places, such as holy water and sacramentals purchased at a basilica gift shop and blessed by a priest, and also natural objects obtained from nature, such as rocks, twigs, branches, soil, and water.

Chapter 15

Conclusion

What I had hoped to accomplish in writing this book was to share with you building blocks for you to create your own practice, to forge your own path of Italian witchcraft. All the threads that make up this beautiful tapestry of an ancient practice are still very alive and relevant to the magically inclined today. I hope to transmit to you my passion for this magical worldview where the mundane, arcane, sacred, and profane blend seamlessly into the tapestry of where we came from and who we are.

I hope my book makes you curious about your ancestors. I hope it helps you see how much your nonni taught you that you weren't aware they were teaching you. I hope my stories stir long-forgotten memories of your own childhood. I hope the book makes you want to cook and learn how to craft. I hope it makes you want to start practicing your customs and traditions and create new customs and traditions to hand down to your children and grandchildren. I hope my book serves as a road map, a guide, a handbook on how to live this beautiful tradition.

Glossary

Abruzzese: (adj.) of or from Abruzzo

Abruzzo: region in central Italy on the Adriatic coast

Altare: altar

Amarena: sour black cherry

Ammazz' i migri: kills germs, antiseptic

Antenati: ancestors

Assabinidica (Neapolitan and Sicilian), **s'abbinirica** (Neapolitan and Sicilian): God bless.

Benedire: (verb) to bless

Benedizione: (noun) blessing

Biscotti secchi: twice-baked dry biscuits

Bonbonniere: sugar-coated almonds in a tulle bag given out as party favors on occasions such as bridal showers, weddings, etc.

Braciole: (noun) chop, as in pork chop

Briscola: card game

Brodo: broth

Ca lu Signuri t'abbinidici (Sicilian): May God bless you.

Candelora: Candlemas

Ce vedimmo (o verimmo) (Neapolitan): We'll be seeing you. See you later.

Ciao: Hello, Goodbye, Greetings.

Commara: Godmother

Compare: Godfather

Corallo: coral

Corno: animal horn or long, red-pepper-shaped amulet; a ward against the evil eye

Cucina: (noun) kitchen, cuisine

Cucinare: (verb) to cook

Cugina: female cousin

Cugino: male cousin

Dialetto: dialect—a version of a language specific to a region

Disinfettare: (verb) to disinfect

Ex-voto: an object used as an offering to a saint

Fattura: spell, curse

Fatture: (plural of *fattura*)

Femmina di casa: homemaker; also implies a respectable woman

Festa: holiday, party, feast, celebration

Feste: (plural of *festa*)

Fettuccia: ribbon

Figlia: daughter

Figlio: son

Genuina: genuine; typically referring to food, as in the genuine article

Gli antichi: the old ones, ancestors.

Il mese dei morti: the month of the dead, November

Impacchi caldi: warm compresses

Maccheroni: pasta

Maga: female magician, sorceress

Mago: male magician, sorcerer

Maleficio: a spell to harm

Malocchio/Mal'Occhio: the evil eye; a spell believed to be cast (unintentionally) by the mere glance from a person who is envious of you

Malvagio: evil

Madre/Mamma: Mother

Mamma mia!: Mother of mine! Exclamation similar to "good grief!"

Minestra di bietola e patate: chard and potato soup

Minestra di verdure: vegetable soup

Napoletano: Neapolitan, of or from Naples

Nipote: niece/nephew, grandchild (depending on context)

Nonna: Grandmother

Nonno: Grandfather

Ossa dei morti: bones of the dead—cookies in the shape of bones

Padre/Papà: Father

Paesana: countrywoman, female from the same town as you

Paesano: countryman, male from the same town as you

Paese: town, word typically to describe one's hometown

Pasta asciutta: cooked pasta tossed in just enough sauce to coat the noodles

Penne: quills, pasta noodles in the shape of quills

Pizza fritta: fried pizza dough

Regione: region. Italy is made up of these 20 regions and their capitals from north to south: Valle d'Aosta (Aosta), Piemonte (Torino), Liguria (Genova), Lombardia (Milano), Trentino-AltoAdige (Trento), Veneto (Venezia), Friuli-Venezia Giulia (Trieste), Emilia-Romagna (Bologna), Toscana (Firenze), Marche (Ancona), Umbria (Perugia), Lazio (Roma), Abruzzo (L'Aquila), Molise (Campobasso), Campania (Napoli), Basilicata (Potenza), Puglia (Bari), Calabria (Catanzaro), Sicilia (Palermo), and Sardegna (Cagliari).

San Michele: Saint Michael

Santucci [SAN-too-chee]: handmade charm bags (amulets or talismans) dedicated to a saint for a specific purpose

Scaramanzia [scah-rah-mahn-zee-ah]: a word, formula, gesture, or action used to ward off the evil eye and bad luck

Scongiuro: spell, charm, exorcism

sci-bendette-Di (Abruzzese): Praise God.

Siciliano: of or from Sicily

Signora: Missus, Madam, a married woman, a lady

Signore: Mister, Sir, a gentleman

Signorina: Miss, unmarried woman, young lady

Spaghetti: little strings, pasta in the shape of little strings

Statte buono/statte bunariello (Neapolitan): Keep well.

Strega: witch

Stregone: male witch

Stregoneria: witchery, witchcraft

Tre-Sette: card game

Vermi: worms—literal and metaphysical

Vongole: clams

Zia [ZEE-ah], **zie** [ZEE-eh], plural: aunt

Zio: [ZEE-oh], **zii** [ZEE-ee], plural: uncle

Zuppa: soup

Acknowledgments

I wish to thank:

My late parents, Rosa and Antonio, for placing me in the care of the people that would go on to teach me all these customs and traditions. Also, for making me attend seven years of Saturday morning Italian school when I really wanted to watch cartoons.

My ancestors: the matriarchs and patriarchs in my family and community for openly and enthusiastically sharing your recipes and magical ways. Your memories and customs will live forever.

Antonina Di Giorgio and Cettina Ragusa for each taking the time out of your busy lives to help me refine my translation and interpretation of Sicilian verses.

My editor, Judika Illes. You were the catalyst to me writing this book. I am grateful for your guidance and support throughout the entire process. You are my idol, my mentor, my literary midwife, and I am honored to call you friend.

My soul mate and husband, Raymond, for your unconditional love and support every day of our lives and for urging me to include my stories.

About the Author

Photo by Raymond Fahrun

Mary-Grace Fahrun was born in Bridgeport, Connecticut, to Italian immigrant parents and grew up in the Italian neighborhoods of Montreal and Connecticut. She describes herself as "an avid keeper of customs, traditions, and secrets" and is an authority on Italian folk magic and folk healing traditions. Fahrun is fluent in the language of her parents and ancestors, Italian (including various dialects), as well as English and French. She learned her craft at the feet of the great matriarchs and patriarchs of her family and community and has been practicing it for more than thirty years. A modern health-care professional and saint magic healer, Fahrun's practice combines skills as a folk healer, psychic, natural health consultant, Reiki master and registered nurse. Her website, Rue's Kitchen, dedicated to the preservation of Italian folk healing and folk magic customs has been online since 1998. Visit her at *rueskitchen.com*.

To Our Readers

Weiser Books, an imprint of Red Wheel/Weiser, publishes books across the entire spectrum of occult, esoteric, speculative, and New Age subjects. Our mission is to publish quality books that will make a difference in people's lives without advocating any one particular path or field of study. We value the integrity, originality, and depth of knowledge of our authors.

Our readers are our most important resource, and we appreciate your input, suggestions, and ideas about what you would like to see published.

Visit our website at *www.redwheelweiser.com* to learn about our upcoming books and free downloads, and be sure to go to *www.redwheelweiser.com/newsletter* to sign up for newsletters and exclusive offers.

You can also contact us at *info@rwwbooks.com* or at

Red Wheel/Weiser, LLC
65 Parker Street, Suite 7
Newburyport, MA 01950